DESIGNED FOR ONE!

120 Diabetes-Friendly Dishes Just for You

NANCY S. HUGHES

Director, Book Publishing, Abe Ogden; *Managing Editor and Project Manager,* Rebekah Renshaw; *Acquisitions Editor,* Victor Van Beuren; *Production Manager,* Melissa Sprott; *Composition,* Circle Graphics; *Photography,* Mittera; *Cover Design,* Vis á Vis Creative Concepts; *Printer,* Versa Press.

Printed in the United States of America

1 3 5 7 9 10 8 6 4 2

The suggestions and information contained in this publication are generally consistent with the *Standards of Medical Care in Diabetes* and other policies of the American Diabetes Association, but they do not represent the policy or position of the Association or any of its boards or committees. Reasonable steps have been taken to ensure the accuracy of the information presented. However, the American Diabetes Association cannot ensure the safety or efficacy of any product or service described in this publication. Individuals are advised to consult a physician or other appropriate health care professional before undertaking any diet or exercise program or taking any medication referred to in this publication. Professionals must use and apply their own professional judgment, experience, and training and should not rely solely on the information contained in this publication before prescribing any diet, exercise, or medication. The American Diabetes Association—its officers, directors, employees, volunteers, and members—assumes no responsibility or liability for personal or other injury, loss, or damage that may result from the suggestions or information in this publication.

⊗ The paper in this publication meets the requirements of the ANSI Standard Z39.48-1992 (permanence of paper).

ADA titles may be purchased for business or promotional use or for special sales. To purchase more than 50 copies of this book at a discount, or for custom editions of this book with your logo, contact the American Diabetes Association at the address below or at booksales@diabetes.org.

American Diabetes Association
2451 Crystal Drive, Suite 900
Arlington, VA 22202

Library of Congress Cataloging-in-Publication Data

Names: Hughes, Nancy S., author.
Title: Designed for one! : 120 diabetes-friendly dishes just for you / Nancy
   S. Hughes.
Description: Arlington : American Diabetes Association, [2017] | Includes
   index.
Identifiers: LCCN 2017026464 | ISBN 9781580406734
Subjects: LCSH: Diabetes--Diet therapy--Recipes. | Diabetes--Nutritional
   aspects. | Cooking for one.
Classification: LCC RC662 .H8353 2017 | DDC 641.5/6314--dc23
LC record available at https://lccn.loc.gov/2017026464

CONTENTS

DEDICATION

To "The Greg"

Sometimes you'd get to enjoy six meals a night; then other times...umm, not so much.

Thanks for your flexibility, your gentle critiquing, and for always being there to listen, no matter what kind of day YOU'VE had—it is all about me, right?

Seriously, thank you for, well...being you!

and

To "The Fam"

Will, Kelly, Molly Catherine, Anna Flynn, Sullivan, Annie, Terry, Jilli, Jesse, Emma, Lucy Katherine, Taft, Kara, and now...River! It's getting trickier to fit all of you around the table. I'll just keep adding extensions!

Love when we "bunch up"!

ACKNOWLEDGMENTS

From my editors to the managing director of books at ADA, Andrea Braxton, Rebekah Renshaw, Victor Van Beuren, and Abe Ogden. You feel like family to me now! Thanks for listening to me *again,* believing in my ideas *again,* laughing with me *again,* but most of all, making yet another book a reality!

Melanie McKibbin, my business manager. Thank you for doing all the things in the office that I don't have the time or the patience or the desire to do! Stay with me, Melanie; you've got a box *full* of "to do" post-its waiting . . . always!

Sylvia Vollmer, my kitchen assistant. Thank you for your high energy, your enthusiasm about each taste test, and your willingness to shop, chop, and clean up . . . over and over again! And, you make sense of my notes to you on the test sheets, too! That's what makes you an integral, much needed, much appreciated part of the team!

We made it happen together, you know!

INTRODUCTION

*D*esigned for One! means cooking for one and serving *one*! This cookbook does not contain recipes that can feed an army of four to six, which can leave you with a week's worth of unwanted (and expensive) leftovers. It feeds ONE!

This book contains 120 budget-friendly recipes for the dinner hour, including salads, nonstarchy sides, starchy sides, entrees, and even desserts!

There's also a "How To" section packed with tons of quick tips on how to shop economically, store properly, and stock up "smartly"! Some of these tips are also included with individual recipes as a helpful reminder!

Then, there is the "Two-For-One" chapter! This is a "cook once, eat twice" approach where a recipe is provided and cooked, half is served, and the remaining half may be used in a variety of ways, such as:

1. Used as a base for another recipe in the cookbook
2. Frozen for a later time
3. Shared with a friend or family member for dinner
4. Simply refrigerated and reheated for another meal

And, finally, even though the book focuses on dinners, what is dinner without an occasional dessert? There's an "Extra Easy Desserts" chapter to satisfy your sweet tooth in a healthy way!

Whether you're just starting out or a seasoned cook, this book will show you that you don't have to have a ton of extra food or expensive leftovers to have fast, great-tasting "comfort" anytime you want it. These "quick-to-fix" recipes are extremely easy to follow and use mainstream ingredients. Also, as with all my books with the American Diabetes Association, there's security in the fact that every recipe follows the nutritional guidelines that have been approved by the Association.

So, pick out a recipe, pull out a spatula, and start cooking. It's effortless, and it's definitely fun!

Enjoy,

n

STORE FRUITS AND VEGETABLES IN GENERAL:

Storing Fruits and Vegetables Together: Don't! Store the fruits and vegetables in separate crispers or bowls at room temperature. Never store fruits and vegetables together. Fruits give off a gas that can ripen and spoil the vegetables around them whether they're chilled or at room temperature.

Storing Vegetables: Store vegetables in bags with a few holes in the bag or open the end of the bag to allow air to flow. Do not crowd vegetables in the crispers; they will spoil faster if packed tightly.

Refrigerating Certain Fruits: It's best to store fruits, such as grapes, berries, and citrus in the refrigerator.

Storing Certain Fruits at Room Temperature: Store fruits such as mangoes, melons, pears, and bananas at room temperature. They will continue to ripen when stored this way.

STORE FRESH VEGETABLES AND FRUITS:

Asparagus: When shopping, look for asparagus tips that are plump and firm, not dried out and wilted. Store asparagus by trimming 1 inch from the bottom of the spears, placing in a jar with 1–2 inches of water, and placing a plastic baggie over the ends.

Avocados: When shopping, avocados should have a bit of "give" to them—still firm, but not rock hard. To pick a ripe avocado, remove the small, stubby "stem." If it is bright green under the stem, it is in good condition. If it is light brown or dried, do not buy it because it will be spotty inside. Store at room temperature for best flavor; it will also continue to ripen stored this way. If only half of the avocado is being used, reserve the remaining half with the seed in place (if possible). Squeeze lemon or lime juice over the exposed avocado, cover the entire avocado with plastic wrap, and gently press plastic wrap directly onto the cut surface of the avocado to prevent discoloration. Refrigerate up to 24 hours. If the avocado does discolor slightly, it is still good. If desired, lightly scrape off any discoloration that may have occurred on the surface of the avocado.

Green Onions: Store green onions by removing the rubber band and by placing the onions in a jar with 1–2 inches of water. Place a plastic baggie over the ends.

Fresh Herbs

Basil: Wash and trim the ends of the basil; pat leaves dry. Place in a container with 1–2 inches of water (as you would a bunch of flowers), and store at room temperature away from direct sunlight, changing water every few days.

Cilantro, Parsley, Mint, Dill, and Tarragon: Wash, trim the ends, and pat the leaves dry. Place in a container with 1–2 inches of water (as you would a bunch of flowers), but store in the refrigerator, covered loosely with a plastic bag.

Rosemary, Thyme, Oregano, and Sage: Wash and trim the ends, place in a single layer between damp paper towels, and cover in plastic wrap. Store in the refrigerator.

Heads of Lettuce: Store a head of lettuce, such as red leaf, romaine, green leaf, etc., by wrapping in several layers of damp paper towels. Place in an opened plastic bag and refrigerate until needed.

Loose Lettuce and Greens: Store loose greens, such as kale, spinach, spring greens, bagged salads, butter lettuce, torn romaine, etc., in their original plastic container. Once the package is opened, fold over the bag and use a chip clip or paper clip. Do not seal tightly; a small amount of air needs to flow. Plan on cooking another recipe with that particular ingredient the same week, toss the remaining vegetables into your favorite soups, or add to your favorite sandwiches or wraps! Kale, spring greens, and spinach make a great "minute" sauté, too.

Mushrooms, Sliced or Whole: Store fresh mushrooms of any variety in an opened paper lunch bag in the crisper or main part of your refrigerator. Do not store them in the container they were purchased in or in a plastic bag; they will become slimy and begin to spoil within a couple of days. There is no need to clean *sliced* mushrooms; they are already cleaned. Clean whole mushrooms with a damp paper towel, but don't clean them until ready to use. Plan on cooking another recipe with that particular ingredient the same week, toss the remaining mushrooms into your salads and soups, or add to your sandwiches or wraps.

Tomatoes: Tomatoes are best purchased when they are in season for peak flavors and texture. Grape tomatoes are the most flavorful year-round. Store all tomatoes at room temperature for the best flavor; they will also continue to ripen stored this way.

SHOP SMART:

Pork Tenderloin: Often your butcher can cut a pork tenderloin to the weight needed. If the butcher is not available, a larger tenderloin may be purchased. When you get home, cut it to the weight needed, freezing the unused portion for a later date.

Beef Chuck/Beef Sirloin: Have the butcher cut the beef to the size you need, or you can purchase a larger cut. When you get home, cut into 4-ounce pieces and wrap individually, freezing for a later use.

Chicken Breasts: Chicken breasts can sometimes be twice as big as needed, so simply cut them in half lengthwise and flatten to 1/2-inch thickness between two sheets of plastic wrap. Wrap the remaining breast halves and place in the freezer for a later use.

Tortilla Chips: Buy snack-size packages of tortilla chips. They stay fresher longer and are perfect for portion control! The most economical way is to divide a larger bag of chips into 1-ounce portions and store in snack baggies.

Frozen Raspberries: For a longer shelf life, it's best to buy the frozen raspberries rather than the fresh. Raspberries (even a small amount) add fiber to your dishes. The frozen variety is a great and convenient way to add fiber and flavor to your dishes any time of the year. They're washed and waiting for you!

Potatoes: If you are having trouble finding a potato that is just the exact weight needed, purchase one that is just a bit heavier. When preparing the recipe, slightly trim the ends of the potato and use your kitchen scale to be accurate. *Note: The scales in your market are not exact; they are to be used for approximate weighing only.*

Hard-Boiled Eggs: You can buy packages of hard-boiled eggs in most supermarkets. They can be found in the dairy aisle.

Gingerroot: There's no need to purchase a big piece of gingerroot in the grocery store; just break off a smaller section of the root.

FREEZE CERTAIN INGREDIENTS:

Raw or Cooked Leftover Veggies: If you have a few leftover vegetables (cooked or raw), toss them in a quart- or gallon-size freezer bag, seal, and freeze. Keep adding to it and over time, when the bag is full, simply add cans of diced tomatoes, some chicken broth, and dried herbs to make a very inexpensive pot of soup! Then, freeze the soup in smaller containers to keep on hand for a quick dish!

Sandwich Bread: Freeze a loaf of sandwich bread in the original plastic package. Remove the needed amount without thawing the entire loaf. The slices separate easily when frozen, too.

Canned Beans: Store the unused portion of canned beans in the refrigerator up to two days or place the beans in a small resealable freezer baggie, seal tightly, and freeze flat in a thin layer. By doing so, it's easy to break off what you need after they are frozen, and they thaw more quickly. You can also run the package under cold water to release the amount you need and continue freezing any unused portion.

Cooked Rice: Leftover cooked rice, whether you've cooked it yourself or it's the pre-cooked pouch variety, freezes well. Freeze in 1/2-cup portions in small, resealable baggies for portion control!

BEAT, FLATTEN, MEASURE, AND MORE:

Beat Eggs in a Jar: Whenever you need to beat up some eggs (making scrambled eggs, for example) why mess up a bowl and a whisk? Crack the eggs in a jar, secure with a lid, and then shake! You can get a jumpstart on the day too by placing the eggs in the jar and refrigerating them the night before so they're ready and waiting in the morning!

Break Noodles: Break spaghetti noodles in half before you cook them. Not only does it make it easier to eat, but it makes for smaller bites, which gives the feeling of eating more!

Control the Heat: When adding jalapeño to a dish, remove the seeds and connecting membrane for a small amount of heat. For a much spicier dish, use seeds and connecting membrane.

Substitute Chicken Cutlets: When a recipe calls for chicken cutlets and they are not available, use chicken breast and flatten to 1/4-inch thickness. Cutlets cook in a fraction of the time. Don't overcook the chicken or it will become tough and dry.

Thaw Frozen Veggies Fast: Thaw frozen vegetables quickly by placing them in a colander and running them under cold water until thawed; drain well.

Thaw Frozen Fruit Fast: Thaw frozen fruits quickly by placing them in a microwave-safe shallow pan and microwaving on high for 15–20 seconds.

Pop a Pepper: Use raw petite peppers as a snack or a crunchy side with your favorite sandwich, or slice and toss them into your salads. They last a long time in the fridge as well! Eat the whole petite peppers—all but the stem! The seeds are fun to eat, and they're mild! Fun munchies!

Grab Some Grape Tomatoes: Keep grape tomatoes on your counter always! They have that "in season" sweet flavor year-round and make a great "grab and go" snack— the perfect finger food.

Grill or Broil More Than One Recipe: When grilling or broiling a recipe, such as an entrée, look for other recipes to accompany that recipe, such as a side dish. You can cook both at the same time, saving steps and energy!

Flatten Your Chicken: Place chicken between two sheets of plastic wrap. Use a meat mallet or the bottom of a can to pound to desired thickness. This not only makes the chicken quicker to cook, but it gives the feeling of more to eat!

Cut Potatoes into Cubes: When a recipe calls for a "potato, cut into 1/2-inch cubes," an easy way to do this is to first cut the potato into 1/2-inch slices and then cut each slice into 1/2-inch cubes.

Spritz a Measuring Spoon: When measuring something sticky, such as honey or maple syrup, lightly coat the measuring spoon first with cooking spray. This prevents the ingredient from sticking to the spoon and allows it to pour easily.

Measure Out a "Pinch": You'll see instructions to add a "pinch" of an ingredient from time to time. A pinch is about 1/16 teaspoon. There may be a 1/16 teaspoon measuring spoon on the market, but they can be difficult to find. There is, however, a 1/8 teaspoon measuring spoon. So just use half of a 1/8 teaspoon amount!

Always Prep First: Prep to make everything run smoother, faster, and with the best results. Put the ingredients you'll need to make the recipe on the counter and chop or measure everything out first before you start to cook the recipe. You'll see how easy it makes your life!

Skillets: Have two medium nonstick skillets on hand. Because these recipes are so quick, the skillet is used a lot. Use one for your entrée and one for your side for a super-quick meal.

Food Scale: Food scales are sold everywhere and can be inexpensive and very, very useful. They're a big help if you're trying to figure out if your meat or poultry weighs 4 ounces, for example!

FRUIT AND VEGETABLE SALADS

Romaine and Creamy Basil Dressing

SERVES
1

PREP TIME
10 Minutes

SERVING SIZE
2 cups

2 cups torn romaine lettuce

1/4 cup finely chopped green onion

1 1/2 tablespoons light mayonnaise, such as Hellmann's

2 teaspoons water

1/2 teaspoon vinegar

1/8 teaspoon garlic powder

1 tablespoon chopped fresh basil

1 teaspoon grated Parmesan cheese

1. Place romaine and green onion on a salad plate.

2. Whisk together the mayonnaise, water, vinegar, and garlic powder in a small bowl. Spoon evenly over romaine and onions, and sprinkle with basil and cheese.

CHOICES/ EXCHANGES
1 Nonstarchy Vegetable, 2 Fat

CALORIES: 110
CALORIES FROM FAT: 80
TOTAL FAT: 9 g
SATURATED FAT: 0.5 g
TRANS FAT: 0 g

CHOLESTEROL: 10 mg
SODIUM: 250 mg
POTASSIUM: 310 mg
TOTAL CARBOHYDRATE: 8 g
DIETARY FIBER: 3 g

SUGARS: 2 g
PROTEIN: 2 g
PHOSPHORUS: 30 mg

Greens with Sour Cream Dressing

SERVES
1

PREP TIME
5 Minutes

SERVING SIZE
2 cups salad plus 2 tablespoons dressing

DRESSING

1 1/2 tablespoons light sour cream

2 teaspoons extra-virgin olive oil

1 teaspoon water

3/4 teaspoon Dijon mustard

1/8 teaspoon garlic salt

SALAD

2 cups torn green leaf or romaine leaves

2 tablespoons finely chopped red onion

Black pepper to taste

1. Whisk together the dressing ingredients in a small bowl.

2. Place lettuce and onions on a salad plate, and spoon dressing on top. Sprinkle with black pepper.

CHOICES/ EXCHANGES
1/2 Carbohydrate,
1 Nonstarchy
Vegetable, 2 Fat

CALORIES: 140
CALORIES FROM FAT: 100
TOTAL FAT: 11 g
SATURATED FAT: 2.5 g
TRANS FAT: 0 g

CHOLESTEROL: 10 mg
SODIUM: 250 mg
POTASSIUM: 37 mg
TOTAL CARBOHYDRATE: 10 g
DIETARY FIBER: 3 g

SUGARS: 4 g
PROTEIN: 2 g
PHOSPHORUS: 6 mg

Sriracha Spinach Salad

SERVES
1

PREP TIME
10 Minutes

SERVING SIZE
2 1/2 cups

2 cups fresh baby spinach

1/3 cup matchstick carrots

2 tablespoons chopped red
   onion

1 tablespoon extra-virgin olive
   oil

1 tablespoon cider vinegar

1 teaspoon sriracha hot sauce

1 teaspoon sugar

1. Combine all ingredients in a bowl. Toss well.

CHOICES/ EXCHANGES 2 Nonstarchy Vegetable, 3 Fat	CALORIES: 180	CHOLESTEROL: 0 mg	SUGARS: 7 g
	CALORIES FROM FAT: 130	SODIUM: 180 mg	PROTEIN: 2 g
	TOTAL FAT: 14 g	POTASSIUM: 505 mg	PHOSPHORUS: 51 mg
	SATURATED FAT: 2 g	TOTAL CARBOHYDRATE: 13 g	
	TRANS FAT: 0 g	DIETARY FIBER: 3 g	

No Toss Spinach and Strawberry Salad

SERVES
1

PREP TIME
5 Minutes

SERVING SIZE
1 3/4 cups

1 cup fresh baby spinach

3/4 cup sliced strawberries

1 tablespoon chopped red onion

1 tablespoon sliced almonds

1 teaspoon canola oil

1 teaspoon balsamic vinegar

1/4 teaspoon sugar

1/16 teaspoon salt (pinch)

1/16 teaspoon crushed pepper
flakes (pinch)

1. Place the spinach, berries, onion, and almonds on a salad plate. Drizzle with the oil and vinegar, and sprinkle with the remaining ingredients.

**CHOICES/
EXCHANGES**
1/2 Fruit,
1 Nonstarchy
Vegetable, 2 Fat

CALORIES: 150
CALORIES FROM FAT: 80
TOTAL FAT: 9 g
SATURATED FAT: 0.5 g
TRANS FAT: 0 g

CHOLESTEROL: 0 mg
SODIUM: 190 mg
POTASSIUM: 233 mg
TOTAL CARBOHYDRATE: 15 g
DIETARY FIBER: 4 g

SUGARS: 8 g
PROTEIN: 4 g
PHOSPHORUS: 74 mg

Cranberry-Pecan Spring Green Salad

SERVES
1

PREP TIME
10 Minutes

SERVING SIZE
2 cups

2 cups spring greens

1 tablespoon chopped red onion

1 tablespoon chopped pecans

2 teaspoons dried cranberries

2 teaspoons extra-virgin olive oil

1 1/2 teaspoons balsamic vinegar

1/2 teaspoon Dijon mustard

1/2 teaspoon sugar

1/8 teaspoon garlic salt

1. Place the greens on a salad plate, and top with the onion, pecans, and cranberries.

2. Whisk together the remaining ingredients in a small bowl. Drizzle evenly over all.

CHOICES/ EXCHANGES
1/2 Fruit,
1 Nonstarchy
Vegetable, 3 Fat

CALORIES: 180
CALORIES FROM FAT: 130
TOTAL FAT: 14 g
SATURATED FAT: 1.5 g
TRANS FAT: 0 g

CHOLESTEROL: 0 mg
SODIUM: 250 mg
POTASSIUM: 51 mg
TOTAL CARBOHYDRATE: 14 g
DIETARY FIBER: 3 g

SUGARS: 8 g
PROTEIN: 3 g
PHOSPHORUS: 23 mg

Asparagus Spear Salad with Yogurt Dressing

SERVES
1

PREP TIME
5 Minutes

COOK TIME
2 1/2 Minutes

SERVING SIZE
4 ounces asparagus spears, 2 tablespoons onion, and 1 1/2 tablespoons dressing

4 ounces asparagus spears

1 1/2 tablespoons yogurt ranch dressing

1/4 teaspoon dried dill

1/8 teaspoon lemon pepper seasoning

2 tablespoons finely chopped red onion

1. Wrap the asparagus spears in several damp paper towels. Microwave on high setting for 2 1/2 minutes or until just tender-crisp.

2. Unwrap asparagus, place in a colander, and run under cold water to cool quickly. Drain well.

3. Serve the asparagus topped with the remaining ingredients in the order listed.

CHOICES/ EXCHANGES
1/2 Carbohydrate,
1 Nonstarchy
Vegetables, 1/2 Fat

CALORIES: 70
CALORIES FROM FAT: 20
TOTAL FAT: 2.5 g
SATURATED FAT: 0 g
TRANS FAT: 0 g

CHOLESTEROL: 5 mg
SODIUM: 250 mg
POTASSIUM: 267 mg
TOTAL CARBOHYDRATE: 9 g
DIETARY FIBER: 3 g

SUGARS: 4 g
PROTEIN: 4 g
PHOSPHORUS: 66 mg

Gingered Carrot Salad

SERVES
1

PREP TIME
5 Minutes

SERVING SIZE
3/4 cup

3/4 cup matchstick carrots

1 tablespoon fresh lemon juice

1 teaspoon sugar

1 teaspoon canola oil

1/4–1/2 teaspoon grated
   ginger, to taste

1/16 teaspoon salt (pinch)

1 cup spring greens, optional

1. Combine all ingredients, except spring greens.

2. Serve in a small bowl to contain the juices or serve over spring greens.

COOK'S NOTE: There's no need to purchase a big piece of gingerroot at the grocery store; just break off a smaller section of the root.

**CHOICES/
EXCHANGES**
1/2 Carbohydrate,
1 Nonstarchy
Vegetable, 1 Fat

CALORIES: 100

CALORIES FROM FAT: 45

TOTAL FAT: 5 g

SATURATED FAT: 0 g

TRANS FAT: 0 g

CHOLESTEROL: 0 mg

SODIUM: 230 mg

POTASSIUM: 302 mg

TOTAL CARBOHYDRATE: 15 g

DIETARY FIBER: 3 g

SUGARS: 9 g

PROTEIN: 2 g

PHOSPHORUS: 33 mg

Spring Green Pea Salad

SERVES
1

PREP TIME
5 Minutes

SERVING SIZE
About 1 1/4 cups

1/2 cup frozen green peas, thawed

1 tablespoon finely chopped red onion

1 tablespoon light mayonnaise, such as Hellmann's

1/4 teaspoon sugar

1/8 teaspoon hot sauce, such as Frank's

3/4 cup spring greens

Black pepper to taste

1. Combine the peas, onion, mayonnaise, sugar, and hot sauce in a bowl. Serve over spring greens. Sprinkle with black pepper.

COOK'S NOTE: To thaw frozen vegetables quickly, place in a colander, and run under cold water until thawed. Drain well.

CHOICES/ EXCHANGES
1/2 Starch,
1 Nonstarchy
Vegetable, 1 Fat

CALORIES: 120
CALORIES FROM FAT: 50
TOTAL FAT: 5 g
SATURATED FAT: 1 g
TRANS FAT: 0 g

CHOLESTEROL: 5 mg
SODIUM: 240 mg
POTASSIUM: 118 mg
TOTAL CARBOHYDRATE: 14 g
DIETARY FIBER: 4 g

SUGARS: 5 g
PROTEIN: 4 g
PHOSPHORUS: 58 mg

Tomato Avocado Salad

SERVES
1

PREP TIME
10 Minutes

SERVING SIZE
1 1/3 cups

3/4 cup grape tomatoes, halved

1/2 avocado, peeled and chopped

2 tablespoons finely chopped red onion

2 tablespoons chopped fresh cilantro

1/4 teaspoon garlic salt

1/2 lemon

1. Combine all ingredients, except the lemon. Toss gently and squeeze lemon over all.

COOK'S NOTE: To prevent the remaining avocado half from discoloring, place the avocado half in a bowl, squeeze with some lemon or lime juice, cover with plastic wrap, and refrigerate overnight.

CHOICES/ EXCHANGES
1/2 Fruit,
1 Nonstarchy
Vegetable, 2 Fat

CALORIES: 140
CALORIES FROM FAT: 100
TOTAL FAT: 11 g
SATURATED FAT: 1.5 g
TRANS FAT: 0 g

CHOLESTEROL: 0 mg
SODIUM: 250 mg
POTASSIUM: 653 mg
TOTAL CARBOHYDRATE: 13 g
DIETARY FIBER: 6 g

SUGARS: 4 g
PROTEIN: 3 g
PHOSPHORUS: 70 mg

Tomato-Cucumber and Blue Cheese Salad

SERVES
1

PREP TIME
5 Minutes

SERVING SIZE
2 cups

2 plum tomatoes, sliced in rounds

1/2 cup sliced cucumber

3 tablespoons finely chopped red onion

4 teaspoons white (or golden) balsamic vinegar

1/4 teaspoon sugar

1/16 teaspoon dried pepper flakes (pinch)

2 tablespoons crumbled reduced-fat blue cheese

1. Arrange tomatoes and cucumbers on a salad plate. Top with the onion and sprinkle with vinegar, sugar, and pepper flakes. Top with the cheese.

COOK'S NOTE: There's no need to toss; simply stack and enjoy!

CHOICES/ EXCHANGES
1/2 Carbohydrate, 1 Nonstarchy Vegetable, 1/2 Fat

CALORIES: 100
CALORIES FROM FAT: 25
TOTAL FAT: 3 g
SATURATED FAT: 2 g
TRANS FAT: 0 g

CHOLESTEROL: 10 mg
SODIUM: 200 mg
POTASSIUM: 414 mg
TOTAL CARBOHYDRATE: 15 g
DIETARY FIBER: 3 g

SUGARS: 10 g
PROTEIN: 5 g
PHOSPHORUS: 51 mg

Icy Spiced Pineapple-Raspberry Salad

SERVES
1

PREP TIME
5 Minutes

STAND TIME
30 Minutes

SERVING SIZE
1 1/2 cups

1/3 cup frozen pineapple chunks

1/3 cup frozen raspberries

1 tablespoon water

1/2 teaspoon grated orange rind

1/2 teaspoon white (or golden) balsamic vinegar

1/4 teaspoon sugar

1/16 crushed pepper flakes (pinch)

1 cup spring greens

1. Combine all ingredients, except the greens, in a bowl. Let stand 30 minutes at room temperature to gradually thaw and absorb flavors. Place greens in a salad bowl or rimmed salad plate. Spoon mixture over greens.

CHOICES/ EXCHANGES

1 Fruit

CALORIES: 60

CALORIES FROM FAT: 0

TOTAL FAT: 0 g

SATURATED FAT: 0 g

TRANS FAT: 0 g

CHOLESTEROL: 0 mg

SODIUM: 35 mg

POTASSIUM: 107 mg

TOTAL CARBOHYDRATE: 15 g

DIETARY FIBER: 4 g

SUGARS: 8 g

PROTEIN: 2 g

PHOSPHORUS: 5 mg

Raspberry Orange Spring Salad

SERVES
1

PREP TIME
10 Minutes

SERVING SIZE
About 1 1/3 cups

1 1/2 cups spring mix or arugula

1/3 cup frozen unsweetened raspberries, thawed

1 tablespoon red wine vinegar or golden balsamic vinegar

1 1/2 teaspoons canola oil

1 teaspoon sugar

1/2 teaspoon vanilla extract

1/4 teaspoon grated orange rind

1 1/2 tablespoons crumbled reduced-fat blue cheese or reduced-fat feta

1. Place spring mix on a salad plate, and top with the raspberries.

2. Whisk together the vinegar, oil, sugar, vanilla, and rind. Drizzle over all and sprinkle with cheese.

COOK'S NOTE: It's best to buy the frozen raspberries rather than fresh ones for a long shelf life.

CHOICES/ EXCHANGES
1/2 Fruit,
1/2 Carbohydrate,
1 1/2 Fat

CALORIES: 140
CALORIES FROM FAT: 80
TOTAL FAT: 9 g
SATURATED FAT: 1.5 g
TRANS FAT: 0 g

CHOLESTEROL: 5 mg
SODIUM: 170 mg
POTASSIUM: 47 mg
TOTAL CARBOHYDRATE: 12 g
DIETARY FIBER: 3 g

SUGARS: 6 g
PROTEIN: 4 g
PHOSPHORUS: 0 mg

RED, YELLOW, AND GREEN VEGETABLE SIDES

Toasted Almond–Ginger Asparagus

SERVES
1

PREP TIME
5 Minutes

COOK TIME
5 Minutes

SERVING SIZE
About 12 asparagus spears plus 1 1/2 tablespoons almonds

1 teaspoon sugar

1 teaspoon Worcestershire sauce

1/2 teaspoon reduced-sodium soy sauce

1/4 teaspoon grated ginger

1 1/2 tablespoons sliced almonds

1/2 cup water

4 ounces asparagus spears, ends trimmed

1. Combine the sugar, Worcestershire sauce, soy sauce, and ginger in a small bowl. Stir until well blended. Set aside.

2. Heat a medium nonstick skillet over medium-high heat. Add the nuts and cook 2 minutes or until beginning to lightly brown, stirring frequently. Set aside on separate plate.

3. Bring water to a boil in skillet over medium-high heat, add asparagus, and return to a boil. Cover and cook 3 minutes or until just tender-crisp. Drain well. Drizzle the soy sauce mixture over asparagus and sprinkle with the almonds.

CHOICES/ EXCHANGES			
1/2 Carbohydrate, 1 Nonstarchy Vegetable, 1 Fat	CALORIES: 100	CHOLESTEROL: 0 mg	SUGARS: 7 g
	CALORIES FROM FAT: 40	SODIUM: 150 mg	PROTEIN: 4 g
	TOTAL FAT: 4.5 g	POTASSIUM: 340 mg	PHOSPHORUS: 104 mg
	SATURATED FAT: 0 g	TOTAL CARBOHYDRATE: 12 g	
	TRANS FAT: 0 g	DIETARY FIBER: 3 g	

Green Bean Broil

SERVES	PREP TIME	COOK TIME
1	5 Minutes	5 Minutes

SERVING SIZE
1 cup

4 ounces fresh green beans, stemmed

2 teaspoons extra-virgin olive oil

1/8 teaspoon garlic salt

Black pepper to taste

1. Preheat broiler.

2. Coat a foil-lined baking sheet with cooking spray. Place the beans on baking sheet, drizzle oil over all, and toss until well coated. Arrange in a single layer.

3. Broil 5 minutes or until tender and beginning to brown.

4. Remove from heat, and sprinkle with garlic salt and pepper.

CHOICES/ EXCHANGES
1 Nonstarchy Vegetable, 2 Fat

CALORIES: 110
CALORIES FROM FAT: 80
TOTAL FAT: 9 g
SATURATED FAT: 1.5 g
TRANS FAT: 0 g

CHOLESTEROL: 0 mg
SODIUM: 120 mg
POTASSIUM: 273 mg
TOTAL CARBOHYDRATE: 7 g
DIETARY FIBER: 4 g

SUGARS: 3 g
PROTEIN: 1 g
PHOSPHORUS: 0 mg

Tangy Italian-Style Broccoli

SERVES
1

PREP TIME
5 Minutes

COOK TIME
5 Minutes

SERVING SIZE
1 cup

1/4 cup water

1 cup frozen broccoli florets

1 1/2 teaspoons extra-virgin olive oil

1 teaspoon balsamic vinegar

1 teaspoon Dijon mustard

1/8 teaspoon garlic powder

1. Bring water to a boil in a small saucepan, add the broccoli, and return to boil. Reduce heat to low, cover, and cook 4–5 minutes or until just tender-crisp. Drain well.

2. Meanwhile, whisk together the remaining ingredients. Serve broccoli drizzled with the mustard mixture.

CHOICES/ EXCHANGES
1 Nonstarchy Vegetable, 1 1/2 Fat

CALORIES: 100
CALORIES FROM FAT: 70
TOTAL FAT: 7 g
SATURATED FAT: 1 g
TRANS FAT: 0 g

CHOLESTEROL: 0 mg
SODIUM: 150 mg
POTASSIUM: 245 mg
TOTAL CARBOHYDRATE: 6 g
DIETARY FIBER: 2 g

SUGARS: 3 g
PROTEIN: 2 g
PHOSPHORUS: 55 mg

DESIGNED FOR ONE!

Balsamic Brussels Sprouts

SERVES
1

PREP TIME
5 Minutes

COOK TIME
5 Minutes

SERVING SIZE
About 3/4 cup

3 ounces frozen Brussels sprouts

1 teaspoon canola oil

3 tablespoons chopped onion

2 teaspoons balsamic vinegar

1/2 teaspoon sugar

1/8 teaspoon garlic salt

1. Place Brussels sprouts in a microwave-safe bowl. Cover and microwave on high for 1 minute to thaw; cut in half.

2. Heat oil in a small nonstick skillet over medium-high heat, cook the Brussels sprouts with the onions for 4 minutes or until tender. Stir in the remaining ingredients and cook 1 minute or until beginning to brown.

**CHOICES/
EXCHANGES**
2 Nonstarchy
Vegetable, 1 Fat

CALORIES: 100
CALORIES FROM FAT: 45
TOTAL FAT: 5 g
SATURATED FAT: 0 g
TRANS FAT: 0 g

CHOLESTEROL: 0 mg
SODIUM: 135 mg
POTASSIUM: 359 mg
TOTAL CARBOHYDRATE: 13 g
DIETARY FIBER: 4 g

SUGARS: 5 g
PROTEIN: 4 g
PHOSPHORUS: 61 mg

Portobello Mushrooms with Shallots

SERVES	PREP TIME	COOK TIME
1	5 Minutes	6 Minutes

SERVING SIZE
1 cup

2 teaspoons extra-virgin olive oil

2 tablespoons chopped shallots (or red onion)

1 (6-ounce) package sliced portobello mushrooms (or caps, stemmed and cut into 1/2-inch-thick slices)

1/8 teaspoon garlic salt

Black pepper to taste

2 tablespoons chopped fresh parsley

1. Heat the oil in a medium nonstick skillet over medium-low heat, add the shallots, and cook 1–2 minutes or until beginning to lightly brown. Increase the heat to medium, add the mushrooms, and cook 5–6 minutes or until tender and beginning to brown.

2. Remove from heat, and sprinkle with the garlic salt, pepper, and parsley.

CHOICES/ EXCHANGES

2 Nonstarchy Vegetable, 1 Fat

CALORIES: 90	CHOLESTEROL: 0 mg	SUGARS: 5 g
CALORIES FROM FAT: 50	SODIUM: 140 mg	PROTEIN: 4 g
TOTAL FAT: 5 g	POTASSIUM: 694 mg	PHOSPHORUS: 194 mg
SATURATED FAT: 1 g	TOTAL CARBOHYDRATE: 9 g	
TRANS FAT: 0 g	DIETARY FIBER: 3 g	

Grilled Okra with Pepper Oil

SERVES
1

PREP TIME
5 Minutes

COOK TIME
10 Minutes

SERVING SIZE
About 1 cup

4 ounces fresh okra

1 1/2 teaspoons extra-virgin olive oil

1/8 teaspoon garlic salt

1/8 teaspoon dried thyme leaves

1/8 teaspoon hot sauce, such as Frank's

1. Heat a medium nonstick skillet or a grill pan over medium-high heat. Coat okra with cooking spray, and cook 10 minutes or until beginning to brown and tender-crisp, turning occasionally.

2. Place okra on a plate. Combine remaining ingredients in a small bowl and drizzle the oil mixture over all.

CHOICES/ EXCHANGES
2 Nonstarchy Vegetable, 1 1/2 Fat

CALORIES: 100
CALORIES FROM FAT: 60
TOTAL FAT: 7 g
SATURATED FAT: 1 g
TRANS FAT: 0 g

CHOLESTEROL: 0 mg
SODIUM: 150 mg
POTASSIUM: 340 mg
TOTAL CARBOHYDRATE: 8 g
DIETARY FIBER: 4 g

SUGARS: 2 g
PROTEIN: 2 g
PHOSPHORUS: 69 mg

Mini Pepper Poppers

SERVES	PREP TIME	COOK TIME	STAND TIME
1	5 Minutes	7 Minutes	5 Minutes

SERVING SIZE
1 cup

1/2 (8-ounce) package petite peppers

1 teaspoon canola oil

1 tablespoon balsamic vinegar

3/4 teaspoon sugar

1/2 teaspoon grated orange zest

1/16 teaspoon salt (pinch)

1. Place the peppers in a small nonstick skillet, drizzle oil over all, and toss until well coated. Place the skillet over medium-high heat and cook peppers 7 minutes or until richly browned and tender-crisp, turning occasionally.

2. Remove from heat, toss with the remaining ingredients, cover, and let stand 5 minutes to cool slightly and continue to cook without burning. Serve warm or room temperature.

COOK'S NOTE: It's great to use leftover raw peppers as a snack or a crunchy side with your favorite sandwich, or to slice them up and toss them into your salads. They last a long time in the fridge as well! Eat the whole petite peppers, except the stem. The seeds are fun to eat, and they're mild!

CHOICES/ EXCHANGES
1/2 Carbohydrate, 1 Nonstarchy Vegetable, 1 Fat

CALORIES: 100
CALORIES FROM FAT: 45
TOTAL FAT: 5 g
SATURATED FAT: 0 g
TRANS FAT: 0 g

CHOLESTEROL: 0 mg
SODIUM: 150 mg
POTASSIUM: 242 mg
TOTAL CARBOHYDRATE: 12 g
DIETARY FIBER: 2 g

SUGARS: 9 g
PROTEIN: 1 g
PHOSPHORUS: 29 mg

Cheesy Chili Pepper Skillet

SERVES	PREP TIME	COOK TIME
1	5 Minutes	8 Minutes

SERVING SIZE
1 cup

1 small poblano chili pepper (about 3 ounces), seeded and thinly sliced

1/4 cup thinly sliced onion

1/3 cup water

1 tablespoon medium picante sauce

1/16 teaspoon ground cumin (pinch)

1 ultra-thin slice Swiss cheese, such as Sargento Ultra Thin

1. Heat a medium nonstick skillet over medium-high heat. Coat peppers and onions with cooking spray, place in the skillet, and cook 6 minutes or until beginning to brown on edges, stirring occasionally.

2. Add the water and cook 1 1/2 minutes or until water evaporates. Remove from heat, and stir in the picante and cumin. Top with the cheese, cover, and let stand 2 minutes to allow flavors to absorb and cheese to melt.

CHOICES/ EXCHANGES
3 Nonstarchy Vegetable, 1/2 Fat

CALORIES: 90	CHOLESTEROL: 10 mg	SUGARS: 7 g
CALORIES FROM FAT: 25	SODIUM: 140 mg	PROTEIN: 5 g
TOTAL FAT: 3 g	POTASSIUM: 348 mg	PHOSPHORUS: 51 mg
SATURATED FAT: 1.5 g	TOTAL CARBOHYDRATE: 13 g	
TRANS FAT: 0 g	DIETARY FIBER: 2 g	

Spinach-Shallot Sauté

SERVES
1

PREP TIME
5 Minutes

COOK TIME
3 Minutes

MAKES
1 cup

2 1/2 teaspoons light butter with canola oil, divided use

1/3 cup chopped shallots (or red onion)

3 ounces fresh baby spinach

1. Heat 1/2 teaspoon of the light butter in a medium nonstick skillet over medium-high heat. Cook shallots for 2–3 minutes or until beginning to brown, stirring frequently.

2. Stir in the spinach and toss until just wilted, about 1 minute, using two spoons to toss as you would a stir fry. Stir constantly.

3. Remove from heat using the back of the spoon. Spread remaining 2 teaspoons light butter over the top.

COOK'S NOTE: Use the remaining spinach from the package by adding it to your favorite soups, salads, or sandwiches and wraps.

CHOICES/ EXCHANGES
2 Nonstarchy Vegetable, 1 Fat

CALORIES: 100
CALORIES FROM FAT: 40
TOTAL FAT: 4 g
SATURATED FAT: 1.5 g
TRANS FAT: 0 g

CHOLESTEROL: 5 mg
SODIUM: 150 mg
POTASSIUM: 178 mg
TOTAL CARBOHYDRATE: 12 g
DIETARY FIBER: 4 g

SUGARS: 4 g
PROTEIN: 3 g
PHOSPHORUS: 32 mg

Jalapeño Skillet Squash

SERVES
1

PREP TIME
10 Minutes

COOK TIME
8 Minutes

SERVING SIZE
1 cup

1 teaspoon canola oil

1/2 cup chopped onion

1 medium sliced crookneck squash

1 jalapeño, seeded and finely chopped

1/16 teaspoon salt (pinch)

1. Heat the oil in a medium nonstick skillet over medium-high heat. Cook the onions 2 minutes. Add the squash and jalapeño, and cook 5 minutes or until squash is tender, stirring frequently.

2. Remove from heat, sprinkle with the salt, and let stand, covered, for 1–2 minutes for peak flavor and texture.

CHOICES/ EXCHANGES
3 Nonstarchy Vegetable, 1 Fat

CALORIES: 110
CALORIES FROM FAT: 45
TOTAL FAT: 5 g
SATURATED FAT: 0.5 g
TRANS FAT: 0 g

CHOLESTEROL: 0 mg
SODIUM: 150 mg
POTASSIUM: 525 mg
TOTAL CARBOHYDRATE: 15 g
DIETARY FIBER: 3 g

SUGARS: 9 g
PROTEIN: 3 g
PHOSPHORUS: 81 mg

Yellow Squash and Browned Onion Sauté

SERVES
1

PREP TIME
5 Minutes

COOK TIME
8 Minutes

SERVING SIZE
1 1/4 cups

1/2 teaspoon canola oil

1/2 cup chopped onion

1 medium sliced crookneck squash, sliced (6 ounces)

1/4 teaspoon sugar

1 teaspoon light butter with canola oil

1/8 teaspoon garlic salt

1. Heat the oil in a medium nonstick skillet over medium-high heat. Tilt skillet to coat bottom lightly. Cook the onions 3 minutes or until beginning to brown, stirring occasionally. Add the squash and sugar; cook 5 minutes or until squash is just tender.

2. Remove from heat, stir in the light butter, and sprinkle the garlic salt over all.

**CHOICES/
EXCHANGES**
3 Nonstarchy
Vegetable, 1/2 Fat

CALORIES: 100
CALORIES FROM FAT: 35
TOTAL FAT: 4 g
SATURATED FAT: 1 g
TRANS FAT: 0 g

CHOLESTEROL: 0 mg
SODIUM: 150 mg
POTASSIUM: 117 mg
TOTAL CARBOHYDRATE: 15 g
DIETARY FIBER: 3 g

SUGARS: 8 g
PROTEIN: 3 g
PHOSPHORUS: 23 mg

Peppery Sugar Snap Peas

SERVES
1

PREP TIME
5 Minutes

COOK TIME
4 Minutes

SERVING SIZE
1 cup

1/4 cup water

4 ounces fresh sugar snap peas, ends trimmed

2 teaspoons light butter with canola oil

1/4 teaspoon lemon pepper seasoning, such as Lawry's

1. Bring water to a boil in a medium nonstick skillet over medium-high heat. Add snap peas and light butter. Cook, uncovered, for 3 minutes or until water is almost evaporated. Do NOT stir.

2. Stir in the lemon pepper seasoning and cook 1 minute or until glazed.

CHOICES/ EXCHANGES

2 Nonstarchy Vegetable, 1 Fat

CALORIES: 90
CALORIES FROM FAT: 30
TOTAL FAT: 3.5 g
SATURATED FAT: 1.5 g
TRANS FAT: 0 g

CHOLESTEROL: 5 mg
SODIUM: 140 mg
POTASSIUM: 150 mg
TOTAL CARBOHYDRATE: 13 g
DIETARY FIBER: 3 g

SUGARS: 4 g
PROTEIN: 3 g
PHOSPHORUS: 60 mg

Hot and Zingy Grape Tomatoes

SERVES	PREP TIME	COOK TIME	STAND TIME
1	5 Minutes	4 Minutes	3 Minutes

SERVING SIZE
3/4 cup

1 cup grape tomatoes

1 1/2 teaspoons extra-virgin olive oil

1/8 teaspoon dried rosemary, crushed

1 1/2–2 teaspoons balsamic vinegar

1/16 teaspoon garlic powder (pinch)

1/16 teaspoon salt (pinch)

1. Preheat broiler.

2. Place the tomatoes on a foil-lined baking sheet. Toss with the oil and broil 3–4 minutes or until beginning to brown.

3. Remove from broiler, toss with remaining ingredients, and let stand 3 minutes to absorb flavors and cool slightly. Serve warm or room temperature.

CHOICES/ EXCHANGES
1 Nonstarchy Vegetable, 1 1/2 Fat

CALORIES: 90
CALORIES FROM FAT: 70
TOTAL FAT: 7 g
SATURATED FAT: 1 g
TRANS FAT: 0 g

CHOLESTEROL: 0 mg
SODIUM: 150 mg
POTASSIUM: 336 mg
TOTAL CARBOHYDRATE: 6 g
DIETARY FIBER: 2 g

SUGARS: 4 g
PROTEIN: 1 g
PHOSPHORUS: 34 mg

Zucchini Wide Ribbons

SERVES	PREP TIME	COOK TIME
1	5 Minutes	2 Minutes

SERVING SIZE
1 1/2 cups

1 medium zucchini (7 ounces total)

1 1/2 teaspoons extra-virgin olive oil

2 teaspoons chopped fresh basil or 1/4 teaspoon dried basil

1/8 teaspoon garlic salt

Black pepper to taste

1/2 teaspoon grated Parmesan cheese

1. Using a vegetable peeler, run the peeler lengthwise down the zucchini, forming flat ribbons.

2. Heat the oil in a medium nonstick skillet over medium-high heat. Tilt skillet to coat bottom lightly. Add the zucchini and cook 1 1/2–2 minutes or until *just* tender-crisp—don't overcook.

3. Remove from heat, and sprinkle with remaining ingredients.

CHOICES/ EXCHANGES
1 Nonstarchy Vegetable, 1 1/2 Fat

CALORIES: 100
CALORIES FROM FAT: 70
TOTAL FAT: 8 g
SATURATED FAT: 1.5 g
TRANS FAT: 0 g

CHOLESTEROL: 0 mg
SODIUM: 150 mg
POTASSIUM: 449 mg
TOTAL CARBOHYDRATE: 5 g
DIETARY FIBER: 2 g

SUGARS: 4 g
PROTEIN: 3 g
PHOSPHORUS: 66 mg

Broiled Zucchini Halves

SERVES
1

PREP TIME
5 Minutes

COOK TIME
5 Minutes

STAND TIME
5 Minutes

SERVING SIZE
2 zucchini halves

1 medium zucchini (about 7 ounces) halved lengthwise

1/2 teaspoon extra-virgin olive oil

2 teaspoons light mayonnaise, such as Hellmann's

1/4 teaspoon Dijon mustard

2 teaspoons panko bread crumbs

1/16 teaspoon lemon pepper seasoning (pinch)

1. Preheat broiler.

2. Place the zucchini halves on a foil-lined baking sheet; drizzle oil over cut sides and broil 4–5 minutes or until beginning to brown.

3. Meanwhile, stir together the mayonnaise and mustard in a small bowl.

4. Spread the mayonnaise mixture evenly over the top of the zucchini halves, and sprinkle with the bread crumbs and lemon pepper seasoning. Broil 15 seconds or until beginning to lightly brown.

5. Remove from broiler, let stand 5 minutes to absorb flavors, and continue to cook without drying out.

**CHOICES/
EXCHANGES**
2 Nonstarchy
Vegetable, 1 Fat

CALORIES: 100
CALORIES FROM FAT: 60
TOTAL FAT: 6 g
SATURATED FAT: 1 g
TRANS FAT: 0 g

CHOLESTEROL: 5 mg
SODIUM: 150 mg
POTASSIUM: 514 mg
TOTAL CARBOHYDRATE: 9 g
DIETARY FIBER: 2 g

SUGARS: 4 g
PROTEIN: 3 g
PHOSPHORUS: 74 mg

POTATOES, PASTA, WHOLE GRAINS, AND MORE

Black Beans with Green Chili Topping

SERVES
1

PREP TIME
5 Minutes

COOK TIME
1 Minute

SERVING SIZE
1 cup

1/2 (15-ounce) can no-salt-added black beans, rinsed and drained

1 tablespoon water

2 tablespoons canned chopped mild green chilies

1 teaspoon fresh lime juice

1 teaspoon extra-virgin olive oil

1/8 teaspoon garlic salt

2 tablespoons light sour cream

1. Place the beans and water in a microwave-safe bowl, cover, and microwave on high setting for 1 minute or until heated through.

2. Stir together the remaining ingredients, except the sour cream, in a small bowl.

3. Spoon the green chili mixture over the beans and top with the sour cream.

CHOICES/ EXCHANGES
2 Starch,
1 Lean Protein

CALORIES: 190
CALORIES FROM FAT: 60
TOTAL FAT: 7 g
SATURATED FAT: 2 g
TRANS FAT: 0 g

CHOLESTEROL: 10 mg
SODIUM: 240 mg
POTASSIUM: 343 mg
TOTAL CARBOHYDRATE: 26 g
DIETARY FIBER: 7 g

SUGARS: 2 g
PROTEIN: 9 g
PHOSPHORUS: 113 mg

DESIGNED FOR ONE!

Lima Beans with Tarragon Mustard Sauce

SERVES
1

PREP TIME
5 Minutes

COOK TIME
12 Minutes

SERVING SIZE
3/4 cup

3/4 cup frozen lima beans

1/2 cup water

1 1/2 tablespoons light mayonnaise, such as Hellmann's

1 teaspoon fresh lemon juice

1/4 teaspoon yellow mustard

1/8 teaspoon dried tarragon (or any dried herb)

Black pepper to taste

1. Combine the beans and water in a small saucepan and bring to a boil. Reduce heat, cover, and simmer 10 minutes or until tender. Drain well.

2. Meanwhile, stir together remaining ingredients, except the black pepper. Spoon over beans and sprinkle with pepper.

CHOICES/ EXCHANGES
2 Starch, 1 1/2 Fat

CALORIES: 210
CALORIES FROM FAT: 70
TOTAL FAT: 8 g
SATURATED FAT: 1.5 g
TRANS FAT: 0 g

CHOLESTEROL: 10 mg
SODIUM: 240 mg
POTASSIUM: 512 mg
TOTAL CARBOHYDRATE: 27 g
DIETARY FIBER: 7 g

SUGARS: 2 g
PROTEIN: 8 g
PHOSPHORUS: 139 mg

White Beans with Basil and Tomatoes

SERVES
1

PREP TIME
5 Minutes

COOK TIME
6 Minutes

SERVING SIZE
1 1/4 cups

1/2 (15-ounce) can no-salt-added cannellini beans, rinsed and drained

1/3 cup grape tomatoes, quartered

2 tablespoons water

1 tablespoon chopped fresh basil leaves

1/2 teaspoon hot sauce, such as Frank's

1/8 teaspoon garlic salt

2 teaspoons extra-virgin olive oil

1. Combine the beans, tomato, and water in a small saucepan. Bring to a boil, reduce heat, cover, and cook 5 minutes or until tomatoes are just tender.

2. Remove from heat, gently stir in the remaining ingredients, except the oil. Drizzle oil evenly over all.

COOK'S NOTE: It's good to keep grape tomatoes on your counter always! They have that "in season" sweet flavor year-round and make a great "grab and go" snack—the perfect finger food.

CHOICES/ EXCHANGES
1 1/2 Starch,
1/2 Carbohydrate,
1 1/2 Fat

CALORIES: 210
CALORIES FROM FAT: 100
TOTAL FAT: 11 g
SATURATED FAT: 1.5 g
TRANS FAT: 0 g

CHOLESTEROL: 0 mg
SODIUM: 250 mg
POTASSIUM: 432 mg
TOTAL CARBOHYDRATE: 21 g
DIETARY FIBER: 6 g

SUGARS: 3 g
PROTEIN: 7 g
PHOSPHORUS: 126 mg

Almond-Ginger Bulgur

SERVES	PREP TIME	COOK TIME	STAND TIME
1	5 Minutes	13 Minutes	5 Minutes

SERVING SIZE
3/4 cup

1 tablespoon slivered almonds

3 tablespoons bulgur

2/3 cup water

1 tablespoon packed raisins, preferably cut in half

1/8–1/4 teaspoon ground cumin, to taste

1/16 teaspoon salt (pinch)

1/16 teaspoon dried pepper flakes (pinch)

1/4 teaspoon grated ginger

1. Heat a small saucepan over medium-high heat. Add the almonds and cook 1 1/2–2 minutes or until beginning to lightly brown, stirring frequently. Remove from saucepan and set aside.

2. Combine water and bulgur in the saucepan. Bring to a boil, reduce heat, cover, and simmer for 10–12 minutes or until water is absorbed and bulgur is tender. If water is not absorbed after 12 minutes, remove lid, and continue to cook 1–2 minutes longer.

3. Remove from heat, and stir in the almonds and remaining ingredients. If time allows, cover and let stand 5 minutes to absorb flavors.

CHOICES/ EXCHANGES
1 1/2 Starch, 1/2 Fruit, 1/2 Fat

CALORIES: 170	CHOLESTEROL: 0 mg	SUGARS: 7 g
CALORIES FROM FAT: 40	SODIUM: 150 mg	PROTEIN: 5 g
TOTAL FAT: 4.5 g	POTASSIUM: 240 mg	PHOSPHORUS: 136 mg
SATURATED FAT: 0 g	TOTAL CARBOHYDRATE: 30 g	
TRANS FAT: 0 g	DIETARY FIBER: 4 g	

Chili-Lime Cob Corn

1 large ear of corn, shucked (7 1/2–9 inches long)

2 1/2 teaspoons light butter with canola oil

1/16 teaspoon chili powder (pinch)

1/16 teaspoon salt (pinch)

Black pepper to taste

1 lime wedge

1. Wrap the corn with several damp paper towels and microwave on high setting for 3 minutes.

2. Meanwhile, combine the remaining ingredients, except the lime, in a small bowl.

3. Remove paper towels, squeeze lime juice over corn, and spread evenly with the butter mixture.

CHOICES/ EXCHANGES
2 Starch

CALORIES: 170
CALORIES FROM FAT: 50
TOTAL FAT: 6 g
SATURATED FAT: 2 g
TRANS FAT: 0 g

CHOLESTEROL: 5 mg
SODIUM: 250 mg
POTASSIUM: 398 mg
TOTAL CARBOHYDRATE: 28 g
DIETARY FIBER: 4 g

SUGARS: 5 g
PROTEIN: 5 g
PHOSPHORUS: 129 mg

No Stir Skillet Corn

SERVES
1

SERVING SIZE
3/4 cup

PREP TIME
5 Minutes

COOK TIME
5 Minutes

1 tablespoon light butter with canola oil, divided use

1 cup frozen corn kernels

1/8 teaspoon smoked paprika

1/8 teaspoon ground cumin

1/16 teaspoon salt (pinch)

1. Melt 1 teaspoon of the light butter in a medium nonstick skillet over medium-high heat. Sprinkle the corn evenly over the bottom of the skillet; do NOT stir. Cook the corn without stirring for 5 minutes or until beginning to brown on the bottom.

2. Remove from heat, stir in remaining light butter, paprika, and cumin. Sprinkle with the salt.

CHOICES/ EXCHANGES
2 Starch, 1/2 Fat

CALORIES: 170	CHOLESTEROL: 5 mg	SUGARS: 3 g
CALORIES FROM FAT: 50	SODIUM: 240 mg	PROTEIN: 4 g
TOTAL FAT: 6 g	POTASSIUM: 290 mg	PHOSPHORUS: 95 mg
SATURATED FAT: 2 g	TOTAL CARBOHYDRATE: 28 g	
TRANS FAT: 0 g	DIETARY FIBER: 3 g	

Fresh Mint Green Peas

SERVES
1

PREP TIME
5 Minutes

COOK TIME
3 Minutes

SERVING SIZE
2/3 cup

3/4 cup frozen green peas

1/4 cup water

1 tablespoon chopped fresh mint

1 teaspoon light butter with
canola oil

1/2 teaspoon grated lemon zest

1/16 teaspoon salt (pinch)

1. Combine peas and water in a small saucepan. Bring to a boil, reduce heat, cover, and simmer 2 minutes.

2. Remove from heat, drain well, and stir in remaining ingredients.

**CHOICES/
EXCHANGES**
1 Starch, 1/2 Fat

CALORIES: 100

CALORIES FROM FAT: 20

TOTAL FAT: 2 g

SATURATED FAT: 0.5 g

TRANS FAT: 0 g

CHOLESTEROL: 0 mg

SODIUM: 250 mg

POTASSIUM: 138 mg

TOTAL CARBOHYDRATE: 15 g

DIETARY FIBER: 6 g

SUGARS: 5 g

PROTEIN: 5 g

PHOSPHORUS: 81 mg

Blue Cheese and Parsley Penne

SERVES	PREP TIME	COOK TIME
1	5 Minutes	10 Minutes

SERVING SIZE
1 cup

1 cup water

1 ounce whole-grain penne,
such as Barilla Plus

1/3 cup grape tomatoes,
quartered

1 tablespoon crumbled reduced-
fat blue cheese

1 tablespoon chopped fresh
parsley

2 teaspoons extra-virgin olive
oil

1/8 teaspoon garlic salt

1. Bring water to a boil in a small saucepan, stir in the pasta, and cook 10 minutes or until tender and water is absorbed.

2. Remove from heat, stir in remaining ingredients, cover, and let stand 2–3 minutes to allow cheese to melt.

**CHOICES/
EXCHANGES**
1 Starch, 1 Nonstarchy
Vegetable, 2 Fat

CALORIES: 200
CALORIES FROM FAT: 100
TOTAL FAT: 11 g
SATURATED FAT: 2 g
TRANS FAT: 0 g

CHOLESTEROL: 5 mg
SODIUM: 220 mg
POTASSIUM: 126 mg
TOTAL CARBOHYDRATE: 22 g
DIETARY FIBER: 3 g

SUGARS: 2 g
PROTEIN: 7 g
PHOSPHORUS: 13 mg

Fresh Lemon Potatoes and Brussels Sprouts

SERVES
1

PREP TIME
5 Minutes

COOK TIME
10 Minutes

SERVING SIZE
About 1 1/2 cups

2 cups water

3 ounces new potatoes, cut into wedges

1/2 cup frozen Brussels sprouts

1/4 cup chopped onion

1/4 teaspoon grated lemon rind

1 tablespoon fresh lemon juice

2 teaspoons light butter with canola oil

2 teaspoons extra-virgin olive oil

1/16 teaspoon salt (pinch)

1. Bring water to a boil in a medium saucepan. Place the steamer basket in the pan, and top with the potatoes, Brussels sprouts, and onion. Cover and cook 9–10 minutes or until potatoes are tender.

2. Toss vegetables with remaining ingredients, except the salt. Sprinkle with salt.

**CHOICES/
EXCHANGES**
1 Starch, 2 Nonstarchy
Vegetable, 2 1/2 Fat

CALORIES: 230

CALORIES FROM FAT: 120

TOTAL FAT: 13 g

SATURATED FAT: 2.5 g

TRANS FAT: 0 g

CHOLESTEROL: 5 mg

SODIUM: 240 mg

POTASSIUM: 695 mg

TOTAL CARBOHYDRATE: 25 g

DIETARY FIBER: 4 g

SUGARS: 5 g

PROTEIN: 4 g

PHOSPHORUS: 107 mg

Cauliflower-Potato Rough Mash

SERVES
1

PREP TIME
10 Minutes

COOK TIME
7 Minutes

SERVING SIZE
About 1 cup

2 cups water

3 ounces red potatoes, cut into 1/2-inch cubes

3/4 cup frozen cauliflower florets

1 tablespoon chopped green onion

2 teaspoons light butter with canola oil

1/8 teaspoon garlic salt

Black pepper to taste

1. Bring water to a boil in a medium saucepan, add the potatoes and cauliflower, return to a boil, cover, and cook 7 minutes or until potatoes are very tender. Remove from heat and drain well.

2. Return vegetables to the saucepan, and stir in the onion and light butter. Mash with a potato masher or a fork to a "rough mashed" texture. Sprinkle with the garlic salt and black pepper.

CHOICES/ EXCHANGES
1 Starch, 1 Nonstarchy Vegetable, 1 Fat

CALORIES: 140
CALORIES FROM FAT: 35
TOTAL FAT: 4 g
SATURATED FAT: 1.5 g
TRANS FAT: 0 g

CHOLESTEROL: 5 mg
SODIUM: 240 mg
POTASSIUM: 871 mg
TOTAL CARBOHYDRATE: 24 g
DIETARY FIBER: 5 g

SUGARS: 4 g
PROTEIN: 4 g
PHOSPHORUS: 116 mg

Buttery Nutmeg Sweet Potato

SERVES
1

PREP TIME
5 Minutes

COOK TIME
6 Minutes

SERVING SIZE
1 potato

1 (7-ounce) sweet potato
2 teaspoons light butter with canola oil
1/4 teaspoon sugar
1/8 teaspoon vanilla extract
1/16 teaspoon ground nutmeg (pinch)

1. Pierce potato with a fork in several areas and wrap in a damp paper towel and microwave on high setting for 6 minutes or until fork inserts easily.

2. Meanwhile, combine remaining ingredients in a small bowl.

3. Cut potato almost in half, fluff with a fork, and top with the light butter mixture.

COOK'S NOTE: If you are having trouble finding a potato that is just the exact weight needed, purchase one that is slightly heavier. When preparing the recipe, slightly trim the ends of the potato, and use your kitchen scale to be accurate. *Note: The scales in your market are not exact; they are to be used for approximate weighing only.*

CHOICES/ EXCHANGES
2 Starch, 1/2 Fat

CALORIES: 160
CALORIES FROM FAT: 30
TOTAL FAT: 3.5 g
SATURATED FAT: 1.5 g
TRANS FAT: 0 g

CHOLESTEROL: 5 mg
SODIUM: 140 mg
POTASSIUM: 482 mg
TOTAL CARBOHYDRATE: 30 g
DIETARY FIBER: 4 g

SUGARS: 7 g
PROTEIN: 2 g
PHOSPHORUS: 67 mg

Tomato Quinoa with Pesto

SERVES	PREP TIME	COOK TIME
1	5 Minutes	10 minutes

SERVING SIZE
About 3/4 cup

3 tablespoons quinoa

2/3 cup water

1/2 cup grape tomatoes, quartered

4 teaspoons prepared basil pesto

1 teaspoon cider vinegar

1. Combine quinoa and water in a small saucepan. Bring to a boil, reduce heat, cover, and simmer 10 minutes or until water is absorbed. Stir in remaining ingredients.

CHOICES/ EXCHANGES
1 1/2 Starch, 2 Nonstarchy Vegetable, 1 1/2 Fat

CALORIES: 220
CALORIES FROM FAT: 90
TOTAL FAT: 10 g
SATURATED FAT: 1 g
TRANS FAT: 0 g

CHOLESTEROL: 0 mg
SODIUM: 250 mg
POTASSIUM: 425 mg
TOTAL CARBOHYDRATE: 27 g
DIETARY FIBER: 9 g

SUGARS: 4 g
PROTEIN: 7 g
PHOSPHORUS: 225 mg

Lemon Dill Asparagus Rice

SERVES
1

PREP TIME
5 Minutes

COOK TIME
4 Minutes

SERVING SIZE
1 cup

1/2 cup frozen cut asparagus

1/4 cup water

2/3 cup pre-cooked whole-grain rice (such as Ready Rice)

1 tablespoon light butter with canola oil

1/2 teaspoon dried dill

1/2 teaspoon grated lemon rind

1 teaspoon fresh lemon juice

1/16 teaspoon salt (pinch)

1. Combine asparagus and water in a small saucepan. Bring to a boil, reduce heat, cover, and simmer 2 minutes or until tender-crisp. Stir in the rice and cook uncovered 1 1/2 minutes or until water is absorbed.

2. Remove from heat, and stir in remaining ingredients.

COOK'S NOTE: If frozen cut asparagus is not available, 1 1/2 ounces fresh asparagus spears (about 6 thin spears) broken into 1-inch pieces may be used.

CHOICES/ EXCHANGES
2 Starch, 1 1/2 Fat

CALORIES: 230
CALORIES FROM FAT: 60
TOTAL FAT: 7 g
SATURATED FAT: 2 g
TRANS FAT: 0 g

CHOLESTEROL: 5 mg
SODIUM: 250 mg
POTASSIUM: 210 mg
TOTAL CARBOHYDRATE: 29 g
DIETARY FIBER: 3 g

SUGARS: 1 g
PROTEIN: 5 g
PHOSPHORUS: 35 mg

Herbed Butternut Squash Mash

SERVES	PREP TIME	COOK TIME
1	5 Minutes	5 Minutes

SERVING SIZE
1/2 cup

1 teaspoon canola oil

6 ounces frozen cubed butternut squash

1 teaspoon sugar

1/4 teaspoon dried thyme

1/16 teaspoon dried rosemary, optional (pinch)

Black pepper to taste

1/16 teaspoon salt (pinch)

1 tablespoon chopped pecans, preferably toasted ▮

1. Heat the oil in a medium nonstick skillet over medium-high heat. Stir in all the squash, sugar, thyme, rosemary, and pepper; cook 1 minute, stirring constantly.

2. Reduce the heat to medium, cover, and cook for 3 minutes or until squash is tender.

3. Remove from heat, sprinkle with salt, and stir to mash. Sprinkle with nuts.

▮ **COOK'S NOTE:** To toast nuts, heat the skillet over medium-high heat. Add the nuts and cook 2 minutes or until fragrant and beginning to lightly brown, stirring frequently. Immediately remove from skillet.

CHOICES/ EXCHANGES
1 1/2 Starch,
1/2 Carbohydrate,
1 1/2 Fat

CALORIES: 200
CALORIES FROM FAT: 90
TOTAL FAT: 10 g
SATURATED FAT: 1 g
TRANS FAT: 0 g

CHOLESTEROL: 0 mg
SODIUM: 150 mg
POTASSIUM: 389 mg
TOTAL CARBOHYDRATE: 30 g
DIETARY FIBER: 3 g

SUGARS: 9 g
PROTEIN: 4 g
PHOSPHORUS: 56 mg

CHICKEN AND TURKEY

Chicken and Red Pepper Mushrooms

SERVES
1

PREP TIME
10 Minutes

COOK TIME
11 Minutes

SERVING SIZE
3 ounces cooked chicken and 1 cup mushroom mixture

1 teaspoon canola oil

1 (4-ounce) boneless, skinless chicken breast, flattened to 1/2-inch thickness

1 (8-ounce) package sliced mushrooms

3/4 cup chopped red bell pepper

1/8 teaspoon dried oregano (or rosemary or Italian seasoning)

1/8 teaspoon garlic powder

Black pepper to taste

1/3 cup dry white wine

1 tablespoon light butter with canola oil

1/8 teaspoon salt

1 tablespoon chopped fresh parsley (or green onion)

1. Heat oil in a medium nonstick skillet over medium-high heat. Cook chicken 2 minutes. Turn and top with the mushrooms, bell pepper, oregano, and garlic powder, and sprinkle with pepper. Cook, uncovered, for 7 minutes, or until beginning to lightly brown, stirring occasionally. Add the wine and cook 2 minutes or until liquid is almost evaporated.

2. Remove from heat, stir the butter and salt into the mushroom mixture and spoon over chicken. Sprinkle with the parsley.

COOK'S NOTE: To flatten chicken easily, place between two sheets of plastic wrap. Using a meat mallet or the bottom of a can, pound to desired thickness. This not only makes the chicken quicker to cook, but it gives the feeling of having more to eat!

CHOICES/ EXCHANGES			
3 Nonstarchy Vegetable, 4 Lean Protein, 1 1/2 Fat, 1/2 Alcohol	CALORIES: 380	CHOLESTEROL: 90 mg	SUGARS: 10 g
	CALORIES FROM FAT: 120	SODIUM: 450 mg	PROTEIN: 34 g
	TOTAL FAT: 14 g	POTASSIUM: 1391 mg	PHOSPHORUS: 480 mg
	SATURATED FAT: 3 g	TOTAL CARBOHYDRATE: 16 g	
	TRANS FAT: 0 g	DIETARY FIBER: 5 g	

Green Chili Pepper Chicken

SERVES	PREP TIME	COOK TIME
1	10 Minutes	7 Minutes

SERVING SIZE
3 ounces cooked chicken

4 ounces chicken cutlets

1/8 teaspoon ground cumin

1/2 lime, cut into 2 wedges, divided use

1/4 cup canned chopped green chilies

1 tablespoon light sour cream

1 tablespoon chopped fresh cilantro

1. Coat both sides of chicken with cooking spray, and sprinkle with cumin.

2. Heat a small nonstick skillet over medium-high heat. Cook chicken 3 minutes, turn, squeeze a lime wedge, and spoon green chilies over the chicken. Reduce heat to medium, cover, and cook 3–4 minutes or until no longer pink in center.

3. Serve topped with sour cream and cilantro. Serve with a lime wedge.

COOK'S NOTE: If cutlets are not available, use a chicken breast and flatten to 1/4-inch thickness.

CHOICES/ EXCHANGES
4 Lean Protein

CALORIES: 160
CALORIES FROM FAT: 35
TOTAL FAT: 4 g
SATURATED FAT: 1.5 g
TRANS FAT: 0 g

CHOLESTEROL: 90 mg
SODIUM: 200 mg
POTASSIUM: 423 mg
TOTAL CARBOHYDRATE: 4 g
DIETARY FIBER: 1 g

SUGARS: 1 g
PROTEIN: 26 g
PHOSPHORUS: 246 mg

Chicken with White Wine Reduction

SERVES
1

PREP TIME
5 Minutes

COOK TIME
7 Minutes

SERVING SIZE
3 ounces cooked chicken and 1 tablespoon sauce

3 boneless skinless chicken tenders (about 5 ounces total)

1/4 teaspoon dried oregano

1/8 teaspoon garlic salt

Black pepper to taste

1/3 cup dry white wine

2 teaspoons light butter with canola oil

1 tablespoon chopped fresh parsley, optional

1. Coat both sides of the chicken with cooking spray and sprinkle with the oregano, garlic salt, and black pepper.

2. Heat a small nonstick skillet over medium-high heat. Cook chicken 4 minutes, turn, add the wine, and cook 3 minutes or until no longer pink in center and wine is almost evaporated.

3. Remove from heat. Place chicken on dinner plate, add the light butter to the pan drippings, and stir until melted.

4. Pour over chicken and sprinkle with parsley or additional black pepper.

CHOICES/ EXCHANGES

4 Lean Protein

CALORIES: 230
CALORIES FROM FAT: 60
TOTAL FAT: 7 g
SATURATED FAT: 2 g
TRANS FAT: 0 g

CHOLESTEROL: 105 mg
SODIUM: 250 mg
POTASSIUM: 515 mg
TOTAL CARBOHYDRATE: 1 g
DIETARY FIBER: 0 g

SUGARS: 0 g
PROTEIN: 32 g
PHOSPHORUS: 309 mg

Sweet Hot Chicken Thighs

SERVES   **PREP TIME**   **COOK TIME**
1   5 Minutes   13 Minutes

SERVING SIZE
3 ounces cooked chicken plus 2 tablespoons sauce

2 boneless skinless chicken thighs (4 ounces total)

Black pepper to taste

1/4 teaspoon grated orange zest

1/4 cup orange juice

1 teaspoon honey

1/4 teaspoon sriracha hot sauce

1/8 teaspoon salt

1 tablespoon chopped fresh cilantro, optional

1. Heat a medium nonstick skillet over medium-high heat. Sprinkle chicken with black pepper; cook 6 minutes on each side or until no longer pink in the center. Set aside on dinner plate.

2. Add remaining ingredients to skillet, except cilantro, and cook 1 to 1 1/2 minutes or until liquid is reduced to 2 tablespoons. Spoon over chicken and sprinkle with cilantro, if desired.

COOK'S NOTE: Before measuring out the honey, lightly coat the measuring spoon with cooking spray, and it will prevent any honey from sticking to the spoon.

CHOICES/ EXCHANGES
1/2 Fruit,
1/2 Carbohydrate,
3 Lean Protein

CALORIES: 190
CALORIES FROM FAT: 45
TOTAL FAT: 5 g
SATURATED FAT: 1.5 g
TRANS FAT: 0 g

CHOLESTEROL: 105 mg
SODIUM: 420 mg
POTASSIUM: 396 mg
TOTAL CARBOHYDRATE: 12 g
DIETARY FIBER: 0 g

SUGARS: 5 g
PROTEIN: 23 g
PHOSPHORUS: 217 mg

Quick Chick Stir-Fry

SERVES	PREP TIME	COOK TIME
1	10 Minutes	6 Minutes

SERVING SIZE
2 cups

2 teaspoons light teriyaki sauce

1/2 teaspoon cider vinegar

1/2 teaspoon sriracha sauce

1/2 teaspoon sugar

2 teaspoons canola oil

4 ounces boneless, skinless chicken breast, cut into thin strips

1 1/2 cups frozen broccoli florets, thawed

1 small red bell pepper, cut into thin strips

1/2 teaspoon grated orange rind

1. Combine the teriyaki sauce, vinegar, sriracha sauce, and sugar in a small bowl; stir until sugar dissolves and set aside.

2. Heat the oil in a medium nonstick skillet over medium-high heat. Cook chicken 2 minutes or until slightly pink in center.

3. Add the broccoli and bell peppers to the chicken, and cook 3 minutes or until vegetables are just tender-crisp. Stir in the orange rind.

4. Spoon teriyaki mixture over all.

CHOICES/ EXCHANGES

1/2 Carbohydrate,
2 Nonstarchy Vegetable,
3 Lean Protein, 2 Fat

CALORIES: 310

CALORIES FROM FAT: 120

TOTAL FAT: 13 g

SATURATED FAT: 1.5 g

TRANS FAT: 0 g

CHOLESTEROL: 85 mg

SODIUM: 430 mg

POTASSIUM: 887 mg

TOTAL CARBOHYDRATE: 16 g

DIETARY FIBER: 5 g

SUGARS: 10 g

PROTEIN: 30 g

PHOSPHORUS: 343 mg

Chicken and Roasted Pepper Long Leaf Wrap

SERVES
1

PREP TIME
10 minutes

COOK TIME
8 minutes

SERVING SIZE
3 ounces cooked chicken, 3/4 cup pepper mixture, and 2 lettuce leaves

1 (4-ounce) chicken cutlet

2 ounces (1/4 cup) roasted red peppers, chopped

1/3 cup no-salt-added garbanzo beans, rinsed and drained

2 tablespoons finely chopped red onion

4 pitted kalamata olives, coarsely chopped

1 tablespoon chopped fresh basil

2 teaspoons extra-virgin olive oil

1 teaspoon red wine vinegar (or apple cider vinegar)

2 romaine lettuce leaves

1. Heat a small nonstick skillet over medium heat. Coat both sides of the chicken with cooking spray and cook 4 minutes on each side or until no longer pink in center. Place on cutting board, let cool 2–3 minutes, and chop.

2. Meanwhile, combine the remaining ingredients, except the lettuce leaves, in a bowl.

3. To assemble, line each leaf with the chopped chicken and top with the red pepper mixture. Eat as you would a hot dog!

COOK'S NOTE: You can replace the chicken cutlet with 1/2 cup cooked, chopped chicken breast.

COOK'S NOTE: You can replace the lettuce leaves with 1 cup chopped romaine and top with the red pepper mixture and chicken.

CHOICES/ EXCHANGES
1 Starch, 2 Nonstarchy Vegetable, 4 Lean Protein, 2 Fat

CALORIES: 390
CALORIES FROM FAT: 150
TOTAL FAT: 17 g
SATURATED FAT: 2.5 g
TRANS FAT: 0 g

CHOLESTEROL: 85 mg
SODIUM: 440 mg
POTASSIUM: 580 mg
TOTAL CARBOHYDRATE: 25 g
DIETARY FIBER: 5 g

SUGARS: 4 g
PROTEIN: 31 g
PHOSPHORUS: 327 mg

Chicken-Cranberry Bulgur

SERVES
1

SERVING SIZE
1 1/2 cups

PREP TIME
10 Minutes

COOK TIME
11 Minutes

4 ounces boneless, skinless chicken breast, cut into bite-size pieces ▪

2/3 cup water

1/4 cup bulgur

2 tablespoons dried cranberries

1 tablespoon roasted, salted, and hulled pumpkin seeds

1/4 teaspoon grated ginger, optional

1/16 teaspoon salt (pinch)

1/16 teaspoon crushed pepper (pinch)

1 1/2 teaspoons light teriyaki sauce

1. Heat a medium nonstick skillet over medium-high heat. Coat chicken with cooking spray and cook 3 minutes or until no longer pink in center and beginning to brown. Set aside.

2. Bring water to a boil in the skillet over medium-high heat, add bulgur, reduce heat to medium-low, cover, and cook 8 minutes or until water is absorbed.

3. Remove from heat, and stir in chicken and remaining ingredients, except teriyaki sauce. Drizzle with teriyaki sauce.

COOK'S NOTE: This is a great way to use leftover chicken. You can use 1/2 cup cooked chopped chicken breast and skip the first step.

**CHOICES/
EXCHANGES**
2 Starch, 1 Fruit,
3 Lean Protein

CALORIES: 370
CALORIES FROM FAT: 60
TOTAL FAT: 7 g
SATURATED FAT: 1.5 g
TRANS FAT: 0 g

CHOLESTEROL: 85 mg
SODIUM: 440 mg
POTASSIUM: 590 mg
TOTAL CARBOHYDRATE: 46 g
DIETARY FIBER: 6 g

SUGARS: 16 g
PROTEIN: 33 g
PHOSPHORUS: 436 mg

Zucchini with Turkey Marinara with Olives

SERVES
1

PREP TIME
10 Minutes

COOK TIME
10 Minutes

SERVING SIZE
1 cup cooked zucchini plus 3/4 cup meat sauce

1 medium zucchini, sliced

1/8 teaspoon garlic powder

4 ounces 93% lean ground turkey

1/3 cup lower-sodium marinara sauce, such as Prego Heart Smart

2 tablespoons water

2 tablespoons sliced ripe olives, drained

1/2 teaspoon dried basil

1/8 teaspoon sugar

1 teaspoon grated Parmesan cheese

1. Heat a medium nonstick skillet over medium-high heat. Coat zucchini with cooking spray and cook 6 minutes or until beginning to lightly brown. Sprinkle with garlic powder and cook 15 seconds, stirring constantly. Set aside on a dinner plate. Cover to keep warm.

2. Cook turkey in the skillet over medium-high heat about 2 minutes or until browned, stirring constantly. Reduce heat to medium-low, and stir in the marinara sauce, water, olives, basil, and sugar. Cook 1–2 minutes or until thickened slightly.

3. Remove from heat. Spoon over zucchini and sprinkle with cheese.

CHOICES/ EXCHANGES
1/2 Starch,
1 Nonstarchy Vegetable,
4 Lean Protein

CALORIES: 250
CALORIES FROM FAT: 60
TOTAL FAT: 7 g
SATURATED FAT: 2.5 g
TRANS FAT: 0 g

CHOLESTEROL: 45 mg
SODIUM: 480 mg
POTASSIUM: 1034 mg
TOTAL CARBOHYDRATE: 16 g
DIETARY FIBER: 4 g

SUGARS: 7 g
PROTEIN: 35 g
PHOSPHORUS: 158 mg

Knife and Fork Turkey-Corn Tortillas

SERVES
1

PREP TIME
10 Minutes

COOK TIME
4 Minutes

SERVING SIZE
2 tortillas

3 ounces lean ground turkey

1/3 cup frozen corn kernels, thawed

1/2 teaspoon ground cumin

2 tablespoons medium picante sauce, divided use

1 tablespoon chopped fresh cilantro

2 (6-inch) corn tortillas

1/2 cup shredded romaine lettuce

3 tablespoons shredded, reduced-fat sharp cheddar cheese

1/2 lime, halved

1. Heat a small nonstick skillet over medium-high heat. Cook turkey 2–3 minutes or until no longer pink, add corn and cumin, and cook 1 minute to heat through.

2. Remove from heat, and stir in 1 tablespoon picante sauce and cilantro.

3. Warm tortillas according to package directions and place on a dinner plate, overlapping slightly. Spoon turkey mixture over tortillas; top with lettuce, cheese, and remaining 1 tablespoon picante sauce. Serve with lime wedges.

COOK'S NOTE: Store unwashed cilantro in a glass or jar of water (as you would a bunch of flowers), but store in the refrigerator. Be sure to rinse sprigs well before using.

CHOICES/ EXCHANGES 2 Starch, 1 Nonstarchy Vegetable, 3 Lean Protein	CALORIES: 330 CALORIES FROM FAT: 70 TOTAL FAT: 8 g SATURATED FAT: 4.5 g TRANS FAT: 0 g	CHOLESTEROL: 50 mg SODIUM: 470 mg POTASSIUM: 173 mg TOTAL CARBOHYDRATE: 37 g DIETARY FIBER: 5 g	SUGARS: 5 g PROTEIN: 30 g PHOSPHORUS: 41 mg

Garden Fresh Vegetable Pasta Toss
page 120

Frozen Banana-Pecan Sandwiches
page 144

Ham, Pepper, and Pineapple Broiler Packet
page 98

Italian Crusted Cod and Spinach
page 74

Knife and Fork Turkey-Corn Tortillas
page 66

Mexican Shrimp with Lime
page 84

Pork and Avocado-Lime Wrap
page 97

Pan-Roasted Salmon with Mango Chutney
page 78

Turkey Patty with Southwest Sauce

SERVES	PREP TIME	COOK TIME
1	10 Minutes	10 Minutes

SERVING SIZE
3 ounces cooked turkey and 2 tablespoons sauce

4 ounces lean ground turkey

1 tablespoon finely chopped green bell pepper

1/4 teaspoon ground cumin

1/8 teaspoon garlic salt

1 teaspoon canola oil

2 tablespoons light sour cream

1 teaspoon barbecue sauce

1 tablespoon chopped fresh cilantro, optional

1. Combine the turkey, bell pepper, cumin, and garlic salt. Shape into a 1/2-inch-thick patty.

2. Heat the oil in a small nonstick skillet over medium-high heat; cook patty 4–5 minutes on each side or until no longer pink in center.

3. Meanwhile, in a small bowl, stir together the sour cream and barbecue sauce.

4. Sprinkle patty with cilantro, if desired, and top with the sauce.

CHOICES/ EXCHANGES
1/2 Carbohydrate,
4 Lean Protein

CALORIES: 210
CALORIES FROM FAT: 70
TOTAL FAT: 8 g
SATURATED FAT: 4 g
TRANS FAT: 0 g

CHOLESTEROL: 55 mg
SODIUM: 270 mg
POTASSIUM: 29 mg
TOTAL CARBOHYDRATE: 7 g
DIETARY FIBER: 0 g

SUGARS: 4 g
PROTEIN: 29 g
PHOSPHORUS: 3 mg

Quick-Baked Potato with Broccoli and Sausage

SERVES
1

PREP TIME
5 Minutes

COOK TIME
7 Minutes

SERVING SIZE
1 stuffed potato

- 1 (7-ounce) red or russet potato, pierced in several areas with a fork
- 1/2 cup frozen small broccoli florets
- 2 tablespoons water
- 1/3 cup turkey sausage crumbles, such as Jimmy Dean
- 2 tablespoons light sour cream
- 2 tablespoons finely chopped green onion
- 1 teaspoon light butter with canola oil
- 1/16 teaspoon salt (pinch)

1. Wrap potato in a damp paper towel and place in microwave. Place broccoli and water in a small microwave-safe bowl, cover, and place in the microwave next to the potato. Microwave vegetables on high setting for 7 minutes or until potato is tender when pierced.

2. Meanwhile, heat a small skillet coated with cooking spray over medium heat. Cook sausage 3 minutes or until beginning to lightly brown.

3. Cut potato almost in half and fluff with a fork. Top with sour cream, sausage, and green onion. Drain broccoli; toss with the butter and salt and place on top.

COOK'S NOTE: If you are having trouble finding a potato that is just the exact weight needed, purchase one that is slightly heavier. When preparing the recipe, slightly trim the ends of the potato and use your kitchen scale to be accurate. *Note: The scales in your market are not exact; they are to be used for approximate weighing only.*

CHOICES/ EXCHANGES
2 1/2 Starch,
1 Nonstarchy Vegetable,
1 Lean Protein, 1/2 Fat

CALORIES: 270
CALORIES FROM FAT: 50
TOTAL FAT: 6 g
SATURATED FAT: 2.5 g
TRANS FAT: 0 g

CHOLESTEROL: 20 mg
SODIUM: 480 mg
POTASSIUM: 1019 mg
TOTAL CARBOHYDRATE: 45 g
DIETARY FIBER: 5 g

SUGARS: 6 g
PROTEIN: 12 g
PHOSPHORUS: 109 mg

Sausage Rice Pilaf

SERVES
1

PREP TIME
10 Minutes

COOK TIME
16 Minutes

SERVING SIZE
1 1/3 cups

1/3 cup turkey sausage crumbles, such as Jimmy Dean

2 tablespoons slivered almonds

1 teaspoon canola oil

1/4 cup chopped green bell pepper

3 tablespoons chopped onion

2/3 cup water

1/4 cup instant brown rice

1/8 teaspoon Italian seasoning or fennel seed

1/2 teaspoon hot sauce, such as Frank's

1. Heat a medium nonstick skillet coated with cooking spray over medium-high heat. Add sausage and almonds and cook 3 minutes or until sausage is browned. Set aside on separate plate.

2. Add the oil to the skillet, and tilt to coat bottom lightly. Cook peppers and onion 2 minutes or until beginning to brown on edges. Set aside with sausage.

3. To skillet, add water, rice, and Italian seasoning. Bring to a boil, reduce heat to low, cover, and cook 10 minutes or until rice is tender and liquid is absorbed. Stir in sausage and pepper mixture and hot sauce; cook 1 minute to heat through.

COOK'S NOTE: For a spicier dish, replace the bell pepper with a large jalapeño pepper, seeds and membrane removed.

CHOICES/ EXCHANGES
2 1/2 Starch,
1 Nonstarchy Vegetable,
1 Lean Protein, 3 Fat

CALORIES: 400
CALORIES FROM FAT: 160
TOTAL FAT: 18 g
SATURATED FAT: 1.5 g
TRANS FAT: 0 g

CHOLESTEROL: 15 mg
SODIUM: 460 mg
POTASSIUM: 220 mg
TOTAL CARBOHYDRATE: 45 g
DIETARY FIBER: 5 g

SUGARS: 4 g
PROTEIN: 16 g
PHOSPHORUS: 106 mg

Sausage and Veggie Tostados

SERVES
1

PREP TIME
5 Minutes

COOK TIME
7 Minutes

SERVING SIZE
2 tortillas and 1 cup sausage mixture total

1/4 cup turkey sausage crumbles, such as Jimmy Dean

1 plum tomato, chopped

1/4 cup chopped red onion

1 jalapeño pepper, seeded and finely chopped (or 2 tablespoons finely chopped green bell pepper)

1–2 tablespoons chopped fresh cilantro, optional

1/4 cup shredded, reduced-fat sharp cheddar cheese

2 corn tortillas

2 teaspoons grated Parmesan cheese

1. Combine the sausage, tomato, onion, pepper, cilantro, and cheddar cheese in a bowl.

2. Coat both sides of the tortillas with cooking spray.

3. Heat a medium nonstick skillet over medium-low heat. Add the tortillas; spoon equal amounts of the sausage mixture on each tortilla. Cover and cook 7 minutes or until cheese begins to melt and tortillas are lightly browned on bottom.

4. Remove from heat, and sprinkle with Parmesan. Serve immediately for peak flavors and texture.

CHOICES/ EXCHANGES
1 1/2 Starch,
1 Nonstarchy Vegetable,
2 Lean Protein, 1 Fat

CALORIES: 280
CALORIES FROM FAT: 90
TOTAL FAT: 10 g
SATURATED FAT: 5 g
TRANS FAT: 0 g

CHOLESTEROL: 35 mg
SODIUM: 480 mg
POTASSIUM: 345 mg
TOTAL CARBOHYDRATE: 30 g
DIETARY FIBER: 5 g

SUGARS: 5 g
PROTEIN: 18 g
PHOSPHORUS: 328 mg

Pepperoni Pasta in a Pan

SERVES
1

PREP TIME
10 Minutes

COOK TIME
9 Minutes

SERVING SIZE
1 1/2 cups total

1 cup water

1 1/2 ounces whole-grain rotini, such as Barilla Plus

1/2 cup thinly sliced green bell pepper

1/2 cup no-salt-added tomato sauce

1/2 ounce turkey pepperoni slices (about 7 slices), coarsely chopped

2 tablespoons chopped fresh basil

1 tablespoon extra-virgin olive oil

1/16 teaspoon salt (pinch)

1 teaspoon grated Parmesan cheese

1. Bring water to a boil in a small skillet over medium-high heat. Add pasta and bell pepper, return to a boil, and reduce heat to low; cover and cook 7–8 minutes or until pasta is just tender.

2. Drain in a colander, and return pasta mixture to the skillet with the tomato sauce, pepperoni, and basil. Cover and cook over low heat for 1–2 minutes or until heated.

3. Place on a dinner plate, drizzle with oil, and sprinkle with the salt and cheese. Do not stir.

CHOICES/ EXCHANGES
2 1/2 Starch, 2 Nonstarchy Vegetable, 1 Medium Fat Protein, 2 Fat

CALORIES: 390
CALORIES FROM FAT: 160
TOTAL FAT: 18 g
SATURATED FAT: 3 g
TRANS FAT: 0 g

CHOLESTEROL: 20 mg
SODIUM: 480 mg
POTASSIUM: 210 mg
TOTAL CARBOHYDRATE: 45 g
DIETARY FIBER: 8 g

SUGARS: 9 g
PROTEIN: 13 g
PHOSPHORUS: 18 mg

FISH AND SHRIMP

Italian Crusted Cod and Spinach

SERVES   **PREP TIME**   **COOK TIME**
1   10 Minutes   10 Minutes

SERVING SIZE
1/2 cup spinach, 1/4 cup bread crumb mixture, and 3 ounces cooked fish

1/4 cup panko bread crumbs

1 tablespoon extra-virgin olive oil, divided use

1/2 teaspoon grated lemon zest

1/8 teaspoon salt

1/2 (6-ounce) package fresh baby spinach

1 (4-ounce) cod fillet, rinsed and patted dry

1/4 teaspoon dried Italian seasoning

1 teaspoon fresh lemon juice

1. Heat a medium nonstick skillet over medium-heat. Cook bread crumbs for 1–2 minutes or until golden, stirring constantly. Set aside in small bowl and toss with 1 teaspoon oil, lemon zest, and salt.

2. Heat 1 teaspoon oil in the skillet, add the spinach, and cook 1–2 minutes or until just wilted. Place on dinner plate. Cover to keep warm.

3. Heat 1 teaspoon oil, and sprinkle both sides of the fish with Italian seasoning. Cook the fish 4 minutes on each side or until flaky when tested with a fork.

4. Place fish on bed of spinach, sprinkle lemon juice over all, and top with the bread crumb mixture.

CHOICES/ EXCHANGES
1/2 Starch,
1 Nonstarchy Vegetable,
3 Lean Protein, 2 Fat

CALORIES: 290
CALORIES FROM FAT: 140
TOTAL FAT: 15 g
SATURATED FAT: 2.5 g
TRANS FAT: 0 g

CHOLESTEROL: 50 mg
SODIUM: 450 mg
POTASSIUM: 474 mg
TOTAL CARBOHYDRATE: 13 g
DIETARY FIBER: 3 g

SUGARS: 1 g
PROTEIN: 24 g
PHOSPHORUS: 231 mg

Knife and Fork Fish Taco with Guacamole

SERVES
1

PREP TIME
10 Minutes

COOK TIME
6 Minutes

SERVING SIZE
3 ounces cooked fish, about 1 1/2 cups vegetables, and 1 tortilla

1 (4-ounce) tilapia fillet, rinsed and patted dry

1/16 teaspoon pepper (pinch)

1 (8-inch) low-carb, high-fiber flour tortilla

1 cup shredded romaine lettuce

1/2 lime, cut into 2 wedges

1 (2-ounce) container prepared guacamole

1 plum tomato, diced

1 tablespoon chopped fresh cilantro

1. Coat both sides of the fish with cooking spray and sprinkle with pepper.

2. Heat a medium nonstick skillet over medium-high heat. Cook fish 3 minutes on each side or until opaque in center.

3. Heat tortilla according to package directions. Top with the lettuce, juice of 1 lime wedge, guacamole, tomato, and cilantro.

4. Break the fish apart, place on top of the vegetables, and squeeze the remaining lime over all. Serve open-faced with knife and fork.

CHOICES/ EXCHANGES
1 Carbohydrate, 4 Lean Protein, 1 Fat

CALORIES: 280
CALORIES FROM FAT: 120
TOTAL FAT: 13 g
SATURATED FAT: 2 g
TRANS FAT: 0 g

CHOLESTEROL: 55 mg
SODIUM: 480 mg
POTASSIUM: 629 mg
TOTAL CARBOHYDRATE: 15 g
DIETARY FIBER: 12 g

SUGARS: 2 g
PROTEIN: 30 g
PHOSPHORUS: 224 mg

Tilapia with Tarragon Butter

SERVES
1

PREP TIME
5 Minutes

COOK TIME
6 Minutes

SERVING SIZE
3 ounces cooked fish and 1 tablespoon butter mixture

1 (4-ounce) tilapia fillet, rinsed and patted dry

1 tablespoon light butter with canola oil

1/8 teaspoon dried tarragon

1/16 teaspoon paprika (pinch)

1/16 teaspoon salt (pinch)

1 lemon wedge

1. Heat a medium nonstick skillet over medium heat. Coat both sides of the fillet with cooking spray. Cook 3 minutes on each side or until opaque in center.

2. Meanwhile, stir together the remaining ingredients, except the lemon.

3. Place fish on dinner plate, squeeze lemon juice over all, and top with the light butter mixture.

**CHOICES/
EXCHANGES**
3 Lean Protein,
1/2 Fat

CALORIES: 160
CALORIES FROM FAT: 60
TOTAL FAT: 7 g
SATURATED FAT: 2.5 g
TRANS FAT: 0 g

CHOLESTEROL: 60 mg
SODIUM: 290 mg
POTASSIUM: 358 mg
TOTAL CARBOHYDRATE: 1 g
DIETARY FIBER: 0 g

SUGARS: 0 g
PROTEIN: 23 g
PHOSPHORUS: 194 mg

Fried-Fast Fish

SERVES	PREP TIME	COOK TIME
1	15 Minutes	6 Minutes

SERVING SIZE
3 ounces cooked fish

1 egg white

1 tablespoon water

1 (4-ounce) cod fillet, rinsed and patted dry

3 tablespoons panko bread crumbs

1/2 teaspoon dried dill

1/8 teaspoon paprika

1 tablespoon canola oil

1/16 teaspoon salt (pinch)

1 lemon wedge

1. Whisk together the egg white and water, add the fish, and turn several times to coat.

2. Stir together the bread crumbs, dill, and paprika in a shallow bowl.

3. Remove fish from the egg mixture, and dip fish in the bread crumb mixture, turning to coat. Using your fingertips, gently press the bread crumb mixture so it adheres to the fish.

4. Heat the oil in a small nonstick skillet over medium-high heat, tilting to coat the bottom. Add the fish and immediately reduce heat to medium. Cook for 3 minutes or until browned on the bottom. Turn and cook 3–4 minutes, or until the fish is opaque in the center. Sprinkle with the salt. Let stand 3 minutes before serving to allow flavors to absorb. Serve with lemon wedge.

CHOICES/ EXCHANGES
1/2 Starch, 3 Lean Protein, 1 1/2 Fat

CALORIES: 240
CALORIES FROM FAT: 110
TOTAL FAT: 13 g
SATURATED FAT: 1 g
TRANS FAT: 0 g

CHOLESTEROL: 50 mg
SODIUM: 280 mg
POTASSIUM: 530 mg
TOTAL CARBOHYDRATE: 7 g
DIETARY FIBER: 0 g

SUGARS: 1 g
PROTEIN: 25 g
PHOSPHORUS: 236 mg

Pan-Roasted Salmon with Mango Chutney

SERVES 1

PREP TIME 5 Minutes

COOK TIME 8 Minutes

SERVING SIZE 3 ounces cooked salmon

1 (5-ounce) salmon fillet, rinsed and patted dry

1 teaspoon canola oil

1/16 teaspoon dried thyme (pinch)

1/16 teaspoon salt (pinch)

Black pepper to taste

1 lime wedge

2 teaspoons mango chutney

1 tablespoon chopped fresh cilantro (or finely chopped green onion)

1. Coat both sides of the salmon with oil. Heat a small nonstick skillet over medium heat. Add salmon, skin side down, and sprinkle with thyme, salt, and pepper. Cover and cook 8 minutes or until opaque in center.

2. Remove from heat. Squeeze lime over salmon, spread chutney over all, and sprinkle with cilantro.

CHOICES/ EXCHANGES
1/2 Carbohydrate,
3 Lean Protein,
1 1/2 Fat

CALORIES: 240
CALORIES FROM FAT: 110
TOTAL FAT: 12 g
SATURATED FAT: 1.5 g
TRANS FAT: 0 g

CHOLESTEROL: 60 mg
SODIUM: 310 mg
POTASSIUM: 570 mg
TOTAL CARBOHYDRATE: 9 g
DIETARY FIBER: 0 g

SUGARS: 8 g
PROTEIN: 23 g
PHOSPHORUS: 228 mg

Poached Salmon with Creamy Cucumber-Caper Sauce

SERVES 1   **PREP TIME** 5 Minutes   **COOK TIME** 4 Minutes

SERVING SIZE
3 ounces cooked salmon and 1/4 cup sauce

3 cups water

1 lemon, cut into 4 slices

1 (4-ounce) salmon fillet, rinsed and patted dry

3 tablespoons plain 2% Greek yogurt

2 tablespoons finely chopped cucumber

1/2 teaspoon capers

1/4 teaspoon dried dill

1/4 teaspoon garlic salt

Black pepper to taste

1. Combine the water and 3 lemon slices in a medium nonstick skillet and bring to a boil over medium-high heat. Add the salmon, return to a boil, reduce the heat to medium, cover, and cook 4 minutes or until opaque in center.

2. Meanwhile, combine yogurt, cucumber, capers, dill, and garlic salt in a small bowl, mashing the capers with a fork to release juices.

3. Remove salmon with a slotted spatula. Squeeze the juice from the remaining lemon slice over salmon, sprinkle with pepper, and serve sauce alongside.

CHOICES/ EXCHANGES
4 Lean Protein

CALORIES: 190
CALORIES FROM FAT: 70
TOTAL FAT: 8 g
SATURATED FAT: 1.5 g
TRANS FAT: 0 g

CHOLESTEROL: 65 mg
SODIUM: 340 mg
POTASSIUM: 587 mg
TOTAL CARBOHYDRATE: 3 g
DIETARY FIBER: 0 g

SUGARS: 2 g
PROTEIN: 26 g
PHOSPHORUS: 231 mg

Tuna and Egg on Spinach

SERVES	PREP TIME
1	10 Minutes

SERVING SIZE
About 3 cups salad

SALAD

1 1/2 cups fresh baby spinach

3/4 cup matchstick carrots

1 (2.6-ounce) pouch low-sodium chunk light tuna in water, drained and flaked

1 hard-boiled egg, coarsely chopped

DRESSING

1 tablespoon extra-virgin olive oil

1 tablespoon balsamic vinegar

1/2 teaspoon dried oregano

1/2 teaspoon sugar

1/4 teaspoon Worcestershire sauce

1/8 teaspoon garlic salt

1. Place spinach on a dinner plate, top with the carrots, tuna, and egg.

2. In a small jar, combine the remaining ingredients, secure with lid, and shake vigorously until well blended. Drizzle over all. Do not stir.

> **COOK'S NOTE:** Pre-cooked hard-boiled eggs may be purchased in major grocery stores, if desired. They are located in the deli aisle and/or dairy aisle.

TUNA AND SALAD WITHOUT DRESSING

CHOICES/ EXCHANGES
2 Nonstarchy Vegetable, 3 Lean Protein

CALORIES: 200	CHOLESTEROL: 215 mg	SUGARS: 5 g
CALORIES FROM FAT: 50	SODIUM: 340 mg	PROTEIN: 26 g
TOTAL FAT: 5 g	POTASSIUM: 362 mg	PHOSPHORUS: 131 mg
SATURATED FAT: 1.5 g	TOTAL CARBOHYDRATE: 12 g	
TRANS FAT: 0 g	DIETARY FIBER: 5 g	

DRESSING

CHOICES/ EXCHANGES
3 Fat

CALORIES: 140	CHOLESTEROL: 0 mg	SUGARS: 4 g
CALORIES FROM FAT: 130	SODIUM: 140 mg	PROTEIN: 0 g
TOTAL FAT: 14 g	POTASSIUM: 0 mg	PHOSPHORUS: 0 mg
SATURATED FAT: 2 g	TOTAL CARBOHYDRATE: 4 g	
TRANS FAT: 0 g	DIETARY FIBER: 0 g	

Curried Tuna Salad on Mango

SERVES
1

PREP TIME
10 Minutes

SERVING SIZE
1 cup tuna salad and 2 1/4 cups mango and lettuce

1 (2.6-ounce) pouch low-sodium chunk light tuna in water, drained

2 tablespoons light mayonnaise, such as Hellmann's

1/2 teaspoon curry powder

1/8 teaspoon sugar

1/16 teaspoon crushed pepper flakes, optional (pinch)

1/2 cup sliced celery

1 cup baby kale and greens, such as Dole Power Up Greens

1 1/4 cups frozen mango chunks, thawed ▮

1. Combine the tuna, mayonnaise, curry, sugar, and pepper flakes in a bowl and stir until well blended. Stir in the celery.

2. Place the greens on a dinner plate, spoon the tuna mixture on top, and sprinkle the mango around the outer edges of the tuna mixture.

▮ **COOK'S NOTE:** To thaw quickly, place mango in a microwave-safe bowl, cover, and microwave on high setting for 30 seconds.

CHOICES/ EXCHANGES
2 1/2 Fruit,
1 Nonstarchy Vegetable,
2 Lean Protein,
1 1/2 Fat

CALORIES: 340
CALORIES FROM FAT: 100
TOTAL FAT: 11 g
SATURATED FAT: 2 g
TRANS FAT: 0 g

CHOLESTEROL: 40 mg
SODIUM: 440 mg
POTASSIUM: 271 mg
TOTAL CARBOHYDRATE: 45 g
DIETARY FIBER: 5 g

SUGARS: 36 g
PROTEIN: 18 g
PHOSPHORUS: 12 mg

Tuna Steak with Sweet Pepper-Ginger Relish

SERVES
1

PREP TIME
10 Minutes

COOK TIME
4 Minutes

SERVING SIZE
3 ounces cooked tuna, 1/3 cup relish, and 1/2 avocado

RELISH

1/4 cup finely chopped red bell pepper

2 tablespoons finely chopped red onion

1/4 teaspoon grated ginger

1 teaspoon white (or golden) balsamic vinegar (or fresh lemon juice)

1/4 teaspoon sugar

1 (4-ounce) tuna steak

1 teaspoon canola oil

1/8 teaspoon salt

Black pepper to taste

1/2 avocado, cut in half and seeded

1 lemon wedge

1. Combine the relish ingredients in a small bowl; toss until well blended and set aside.

2. Brush both sides of the tuna with oil. Heat a grill pan or skillet over medium-high heat. Cook tuna 2 minutes on each side or until very pink in center. Do NOT overcook or it will be tough and dry. Sprinkle tuna with salt and pepper.

3. Place the avocado slices first on the dinner plate. Squeeze the lemon over avocado, and top with the tuna and relish.

COOK'S NOTE: To prevent the remaining avocado half from discoloring, place the avocado half in a bowl, squeeze with lemon or lime juice, cover with plastic wrap, and refrigerate overnight.

CHOICES/ EXCHANGES

1/2 Fruit,
1 Nonstarchy Vegetable,
4 Lean Protein, 2 Fat

CALORIES: 310
CALORIES FROM FAT: 140
TOTAL FAT: 16 g
SATURATED FAT: 2 g
TRANS FAT: 0 g

CHOLESTEROL: 45 mg
SODIUM: 350 mg
POTASSIUM: 963 mg
TOTAL CARBOHYDRATE: 14 g
DIETARY FIBER: 6 g

SUGARS: 6 g
PROTEIN: 30 g
PHOSPHORUS: 368 mg

Shrimp with Sun-Dried Tomatoes and Capers

SERVES 1

PREP TIME 10 Minutes

COOK TIME 4 Minutes

SERVING SIZE 3/4 cup

1 tablespoon extra-svirgin olive oil, divided use

4 ounces medium raw peeled shrimp

1 teaspoon chopped sun-dried tomatoes (not packed in oil)

1/4 teaspoon dried oregano

1 teaspoon capers, drained

1 tablespoon light butter with canola oil

1/8 teaspoon garlic powder

1/16 teaspoon salt (pinch)

1 lemon wedge

1. Heat 1 teaspoon oil in a medium nonstick skillet over medium heat. Add shrimp, tomatoes, and oregano; cook 4 minutes or until shrimp is opaque in center, stirring frequently. Stir the capers into shrimp mixture and cook 15 seconds, stirring constantly.

2. Remove from heat, and stir in the light butter, garlic powder, 2 teaspoons oil, and salt.

3. Squeeze lemon juice over all.

> **COOK'S NOTE:** You might want to serve in a small bowl to contain the flavorful juices.

CHOICES/ EXCHANGES
2 Lean Protein, 3 1/2 Fat

CALORIES: 260
CALORIES FROM FAT: 180
TOTAL FAT: 20 g
SATURATED FAT: 4 g
TRANS FAT: 0 g

CHOLESTEROL: 150 mg
SODIUM: 480 mg
POTASSIUM: 78 mg
TOTAL CARBOHYDRATE: 2 g
DIETARY FIBER: 0 g

SUGARS: 1 g
PROTEIN: 16 g
PHOSPHORUS: 8 mg

Mexican Shrimp with Lime

SERVES	PREP TIME	COOK TIME
1	10 Minutes	6 Minutes

SERVING SIZE
1 cup

1/4 cup chopped onion
4 ounces peeled raw shrimp
1 1/2 tablespoons light butter
3/4 teaspoon chili powder
1/2 teaspoon ground cumin
1/4 teaspoon lemon pepper
   seasoning
1 tablespoon chopped fresh
   cilantro, optional
1 lime, halved

1. Heat a medium nonstick skillet over medium heat. Coat the onions with cooking spray and cook 2 minutes. Coat the shrimp with cooking spray, add to the onion, and cook mixture for 4 minutes or until shrimp are opaque in center. Remove from heat.

2. Stir in the remaining ingredients, except the lime. Squeeze the lime juice over all. Cover and let stand 2 minutes to absorb flavors.

CHOICES/ EXCHANGES
1/2 Carbohydrate,
2 Lean Protein,
1 1/2 Fat

CALORIES: 190
CALORIES FROM FAT: 80
TOTAL FAT: 9 g
SATURATED FAT: 3 g
TRANS FAT: 0 g

CHOLESTEROL: 150 mg
SODIUM: 460 mg
POTASSIUM: 147 mg
TOTAL CARBOHYDRATE: 9 g
DIETARY FIBER: 2 g

SUGARS: 2 g
PROTEIN: 16 g
PHOSPHORUS: 24 mg

Lemony Shrimp Salad on Avocado

SERVES
1

PREP TIME
10 Minutes

COOK TIME
5 Minutes

SERVING SIZE
1 cup shrimp mixture plus 1/2 cup avocado

1/2 cup water

4 ounces peeled raw shrimp

1 tablespoon light mayonnaise, such as Hellmann's

1/2 teaspoon grated lemon rind

2 tablespoons fresh lemon juice, divided use

1/4 teaspoon seafood seasoning, such as Old Bay

1/4 cup chopped celery

2 tablespoons chopped red onion

1/2 avocado, peeled and sliced

1. Bring water to a boil in a small saucepan, add the shrimp, and return to a boil. Reduce heat to medium-low, cover, and cook 4 minutes or until opaque in center. Drain and let stand to cool, about 5 minutes.

2. Meanwhile, whisk together the mayonnaise, lemon rind, 1 tablespoon lemon juice, and seafood seasoning in a bowl. Stir in the shrimp, celery, and onion.

3. Arrange the avocado slices on a dinner plate. Sprinkle 1 tablespoon lemon juice over the slices and top with the shrimp salad.

COOK'S NOTE: Squeeze lemon or lime juice over remaining avocado half. Cover with plastic wrap, pressing down in the center to remove as much air as possible and refrigerate. Use next day for peak flavor and texture. If discoloration does occur, simply remove it by gently running a spoon across to remove it, if desired.

CHOICES/ EXCHANGES
1 Carbohydrate, 2 Lean Protein, 2 1/2 Fat

CALORIES: 260
CALORIES FROM FAT: 150
TOTAL FAT: 17 g
SATURATED FAT: 2.5 g
TRANS FAT: 0 g

CHOLESTEROL: 150 mg
SODIUM: 470 mg
POTASSIUM: 473 mg
TOTAL CARBOHYDRATE: 13 g
DIETARY FIBER: 6 g

SUGARS: 2 g
PROTEIN: 17 g
PHOSPHORUS: 51 mg

BEEF AND PORK

Sirloin Steak and Peppers with Horseradish Sauce

SERVES
1

PREP TIME
10 Minutes

COOK TIME
8 Minutes

SERVING SIZE
3 ounces cooked beef, 1 cup vegetables, and 2 tablespoons sauce

1 teaspoon canola oil

4 ounces boneless top sirloin steak

1 small green bell pepper, thinly sliced

1/2 cup chopped onion

2 tablespoons light sour cream

1 teaspoon grated prepared horseradish

1/8 teaspoon Worcestershire sauce

1 tablespoon water

1/8 teaspoon salt

Black pepper to taste

1. Heat the oil in a medium nonstick skillet over medium-high heat; tilt skillet to coat bottom. Add beef and sprinkle peppers and onions around the beef. Cook 4 minutes, turn beef and stir vegetables, and cook an additional 4 minutes or to desired doneness of beef.

2. Meanwhile, combine the sour cream, horseradish, and Worcestershire sauce in a small bowl.

3. Place beef on dinner plate. Add water to vegetables in skillet, stir, and spoon vegetables around the beef. Sprinkle evenly with salt and pepper; serve with sauce.

COOK'S NOTE: Have the butcher cut the beef to the size you need, or you can purchase a larger cut. Cut into 4-ounce pieces, wrap individually, and freeze for later use.

CHOICES/ EXCHANGES

3 Nonstarchy Vegetable, 3 Lean Protein, 1 Fat

CALORIES: 250
CALORIES FROM FAT: 100
TOTAL FAT: 11 g
SATURATED FAT: 3.5 g
TRANS FAT: 0 g

CHOLESTEROL: 65 mg
SODIUM: 390 mg
POTASSIUM: 521 mg
TOTAL CARBOHYDRATE: 15 g
DIETARY FIBER: 3 g

SUGARS: 7 g
PROTEIN: 23 g
PHOSPHORUS: 205 mg

Skillet Steak with Rich Pan Sauce

SERVES	PREP TIME	COOK TIME
1	5 Minutes	8 Minutes

SERVING SIZE
3 ounces cooked beef and 1 tablespoon sauce

4 ounces boneless sirloin
  steak

1/2 teaspoon instant coffee
  granules

1/8 teaspoon black pepper

1/4 cup water

1 teaspoon ketchup

1/4 teaspoon Worcestershire
  sauce

1/8 teaspoon garlic salt

1 teaspoon canola oil

1. Coat both sides of the beef with the coffee granules and pepper, pressing down with your fingertips to adhere.

2. Combine the remaining ingredients, except the oil, in a small bowl and set aside.

3. Heat the oil in a small skillet over medium-high heat. Cook the beef 4 minutes on each side or until pink in center. Don't overcook or it will be tough. Place on dinner plate.

4. Add the ketchup mixture to the pan residue in the skillet, cook 1 1/2 minutes or until reduced to 1 tablespoon liquid, stirring frequently. Pour over steak and top with additional black pepper, if desired.

COOK'S NOTE: Ask your butcher to cut the beef to the weight you need. If a butcher is unavailable, purchase a larger piece and cut into smaller pieces, about 4 ounces each, and freeze individually in plastic wrap for a later use.

**CHOICES/
EXCHANGES**
3 Lean Protein, 1 Fat

CALORIES: 180	CHOLESTEROL: 55 mg	SUGARS: 1 g
CALORIES FROM FAT: 80	SODIUM: 230 mg	PROTEIN: 21 g
TOTAL FAT: 9 g	POTASSIUM: 339 mg	PHOSPHORUS: 168 mg
SATURATED FAT: 2 g	TOTAL CARBOHYDRATE: 3 g	
TRANS FAT: 0 g	DIETARY FIBER: 0 g	

Sirloin Strips with Blue Cheese Rotini

SERVES	PREP TIME	COOK TIME
1	10 Minutes	10 Minutes

SERVING SIZE
3 ounces cooked beef and about 1 1/4 cups pasta mixture

2 ounces whole-grain rotini, such as Barilla Plus

1/2 teaspoon canola oil

4 ounces boneless top sirloin steak, thinly sliced ▮

3 tablespoons crumbled reduced-fat blue cheese

2 tablespoons finely chopped green onion

1/16 teaspoon dried rosemary (pinch)

1/16 teaspoon salt (pinch)

Black pepper to taste

1. Cook pasta according to package directions.

2. Meanwhile, heat the oil in a medium nonstick skillet over medium-high heat. Add beef and cook 2 minutes or until slightly pink in center. Don't overcook or it will be tough.

3. Toss the drained pasta with the cheese, onions, and rosemary; top with the beef and sprinkle with salt and pepper.

▮ **COOK'S NOTE:** Have the butcher cut the beef weight you need, if possible. Otherwise, buy a larger piece, and cut into 4-ounce pieces. Freeze individually.

CHOICES/ EXCHANGES
2 1/2 Starch, 4 Lean Protein, 1/2 Fat

CALORIES: 390
CALORIES FROM FAT: 100
TOTAL FAT: 12 g
SATURATED FAT: 4.5 g
TRANS FAT: 0 g

CHOLESTEROL: 65 mg
SODIUM: 480 mg
POTASSIUM: 303 mg
TOTAL CARBOHYDRATE: 40 g
DIETARY FIBER: 6 g

SUGARS: 2 g
PROTEIN: 35 g
PHOSPHORUS: 166 mg

Mediterranean Unstuffed Peppers

SERVES
1

PREP TIME
10 Minutes

COOK TIME
12 Minutes

SERVING SIZE
1 1/4 cup beef mixture plus 1 pepper

3 ounces 93% lean ground beef

1/4 cup chopped onion

1 1/2 tablespoons roasted, salted, and hulled pumpkin seeds

1/2 cup water

1/3 cup cooked brown rice

3 tablespoons no-salt-added tomato sauce

2 tablespoons raisins

1/2 teaspoon ground cinnamon

1 medium green or red bell pepper, halved lengthwise and seeded

1/8 teaspoon salt

2 tablespoons 2% plain Greek yogurt

1. Heat a medium nonstick skillet over medium-high heat. Cook the beef and onion for 3 minutes, stirring frequently. Add the pumpkin seeds; cook 2 minutes. Stir in the water, rice, tomato sauce, raisins, and cinnamon. Reduce heat to low, cover, and cook 4 minutes to blend flavors and thicken slightly.

2. Meanwhile, place the pepper halves on a microwave-safe plate, cover, and microwave on high setting for 2–3 minutes or until peppers are tender.

3. Turn the peppers over. Stir the salt into the beef mixture and spoon into the pepper halves. Top with yogurt.

COOK'S NOTE: This is a great way to use leftover rice, but if you don't have any on hand, use the frozen whole-grain rice or a pouch of whole-grain rice, such as Ready Rice (unseasoned variety). Freeze remaining rice for later use. You may want to freeze the pouch variety in 1/2-cup portions—for portion control.

COOK'S NOTE: Freeze left-over tomato sauce in a small baggie, lying flat, for later use. Freezing flat allows you to break off a piece at a time rather than having to thaw it all and waste a portion of it. It's easier to thaw, too because it is so thin.

CHOICES/ EXCHANGES
1 Starch, 1 Fruit, 3 Nonstarchy Vegetable, 3 Lean Protein, 1 Fat

CALORIES: 390
CALORIES FROM FAT: 120
TOTAL FAT: 13 g
SATURATED FAT: 4.5 g
TRANS FAT: 0 g

CHOLESTEROL: 55 mg
SODIUM: 410 mg
POTASSIUM: 664 mg
TOTAL CARBOHYDRATE: 45 g
DIETARY FIBER: 6 g

SUGARS: 23 g
PROTEIN: 27 g
PHOSPHORUS: 219 mg

Smoky Beef and Romaine Tortilla Wrap

SERVES
1

PREP TIME
10 Minutes

COOK TIME
3 Minutes

SERVING
3/4 cup beef mixture, 3/4 cup lettuce, and 1 tortilla

4 ounces 93% lean ground beef

1 tablespoon water

1/2 teaspoon ground cumin

2 teaspoons barbecue sauce

1/2 teaspoon Worcestershire sauce

1 (8-inch) low-carb, high-fiber flour tortilla, warmed

3/4 cup shredded romaine lettuce

2 tablespoons finely chopped red onion

1 lime wedge

1. Heat a small nonstick skillet coated with cooking spray over medium-high heat. Cook beef 2–3 minutes or until browned, stirring frequently.

2. Remove from heat, and stir in the water, cumin, barbecue sauce, and Worcestershire sauce.

3. Place the tortilla on a dinner plate, place the lettuce down the center of the tortilla, and top with the onion and the beef mixture. Squeeze lime juice over all. Roll up and cut in half.

CHOICES/ EXCHANGES
1 Starch, 1 Nonstarchy Vegetable, 3 Lean Protein, 1 Fat

CALORIES: 290
CALORIES FROM FAT: 90
TOTAL FAT: 10 g
SATURATED FAT: 4.5 g
TRANS FAT: 0 g

CHOLESTEROL: 70 mg
SODIUM: 450 mg
POTASSIUM: 128 mg
TOTAL CARBOHYDRATE: 20 g
DIETARY FIBER: 7 g

SUGARS: 5 g
PROTEIN: 30 g
PHOSPHORUS: 21 mg

Microwave Mug Meatloaf

SERVES	PREP TIME	COOK TIME	STAND TIME
1	5 Minutes	5 Minutes	5 minutes

SERVING SIZE
1 cup

4 ounces 93% lean ground beef

1 1/2 tablespoons picante sauce, divided use

1 egg white

2 tablespoons quick-cooking oats

Black pepper to taste

1 teaspoon ketchup

1. Combine the beef, 1 tablespoon picante sauce, egg white, oats, and pepper in a bowl. Coat a coffee mug or custard cup with cooking spray. Place the beef mixture in the cup; cover and microwave on high for 3 minutes.

2. Meanwhile, stir together remaining 1 1/2 teaspoons picante sauce and ketchup.

3. Remove from microwave, and spoon the ketchup mixture on the top. Let stand a full 5 minutes to absorb flavors and develop texture.

COOK'S NOTE: Don't skip this step. The beef will continue to cook without drying out, the texture becomes firmer and tightens, and the flavors develop during the standing time.

CHOICES/ EXCHANGES
1 Carbohydrate, 4 Lean Protein

CALORIES: 240
CALORIES FROM FAT: 80
TOTAL FAT: 9 g
SATURATED FAT: 4 g
TRANS FAT: 0 g

CHOLESTEROL: 70 mg
SODIUM: 380 mg
POTASSIUM: 120 mg
TOTAL CARBOHYDRATE: 12 g
DIETARY FIBER: 1 g

SUGARS: 3 g
PROTEIN: 28 g
PHOSPHORUS: 64 mg

Chili Beef and Beans

SERVES
1

PREP TIME
5 Minutes

COOK TIME
9 Minutes

SERVING SIZE
1 1/2 cups

4 ounce 93% lean ground beef

1/2 (15-ounce) can no-salt-added black beans, rinsed and drained

1/2 cup water

3 tablespoons medium picante sauce

1 1/4 teaspoons sugar

1 teaspoon ground cumin

1/2 teaspoon chili powder

1/2 teaspoon balsamic vinegar

1. Heat a medium nonstick skillet over medium-high heat. Cook the beef 2 minutes or until beginning to brown. Stir in the remaining ingredients. Bring to a boil and cook 4 minutes or until thickened slightly.

2. Remove from heat, cover, and let stand 3 minutes to absorb flavors. Serve in a bowl to contain the flavorful juices.

CHOICES/ EXCHANGES
1 1/2 Starch,
1/2 Carbohydrate,
4 Lean Protein

CALORIES: 330
CALORIES FROM FAT: 70
TOTAL FAT: 8 g
SATURATED FAT: 3.5 g
TRANS FAT: 0 g

CHOLESTEROL: 70 mg
SODIUM: 480 mg
POTASSIUM: 506 mg
TOTAL CARBOHYDRATE: 30 g
DIETARY FIBER: 12 g

SUGARS: 9 g
PROTEIN: 33 g
PHOSPHORUS: 146 mg

Pork Chop with Balsamic Raspberry Sauce

SERVES
1

PREP TIME
5 Minutes

COOK TIME
10 Minutes

SERVING SIZE
3 ounces cooked pork plus 1/4 cup sauce

1 teaspoon canola oil

1 (4-ounce) boneless pork chop

1/4 teaspoon dried rosemary, crumbled

1/3 cup frozen unsweetened raspberries

2 tablespoons water

1 1/2 teaspoons sugar

1 teaspoon balsamic vinegar

1/4 teaspoon Worcestershire sauce

1/16 teaspoon salt (pinch)

1. Heat the oil in a small nonstick skillet over medium-high heat. Sprinkle both sides of the pork with the rosemary. Cook pork 4 minutes on each side or until slightly pink in center. Set aside on dinner plate.

2. Add the remaining ingredients, except the salt, to the skillet, bring to a boil over medium-high heat and cook 1 minute or until it reduces to 1/4 cup.

3. Spoon around the pork chop. Sprinkle with the salt.

COOK'S NOTE: Raspberries (even a small amount) add fiber to your dishes. The frozen variety is a great convenient way to add fiber and flavor to your dishes any time of the year. They're prepped and waiting for you!

CHOICES/ EXCHANGES

1/2 Fruit,
1/2 Carbohydrate,
2 Lean Protein,
1 1/2 Fat

CALORIES: 210
CALORIES FROM FAT: 90
TOTAL FAT: 10 g
SATURATED FAT: 2 g
TRANS FAT: 0 g

CHOLESTEROL: 55 mg
SODIUM: 200 mg
POTASSIUM: 286 mg
TOTAL CARBOHYDRATE: 12 g
DIETARY FIBER: 2 g

SUGARS: 9 g
PROTEIN: 19 g
PHOSPHORUS: 156 mg

Pork Chop with Pan Sauce

SERVES
1

PREP TIME
5 Minutes

COOK TIME
9 Minutes

SERVING SIZE
3 ounces cooked pork

1/8 teaspoon dried thyme

1/8 teaspoon onion powder

1/16 teaspoon black pepper (pinch)

1 (4-ounce) boneless pork chop

1 teaspoon canola oil

3 tablespoons water

1/4 teaspoon Worcestershire sauce

1/16 teaspoon salt (pinch)

1. Combine the thyme, onion powder, and pepper in a small bowl. Sprinkle evenly over both sides of the pork chop.

2. Heat the oil in a small nonstick skillet over medium-high heat, and tilt skillet to lightly coat bottom. Cook pork 4 minutes on each side or until slightly pink in center. Set aside on dinner plate.

3. Add the water and Worcestershire sauce to the skillet, stir, and cook 30–45 seconds or until reduced to 2 teaspoons liquid.

4. Spoon over the pork and sprinkle with the salt.

CHOICES/ EXCHANGES

3 Lean Protein, 1 Fat

CALORIES: 160

CALORIES FROM FAT: 90

TOTAL FAT: 10 g

SATURATED FAT: 2 g

TRANS FAT: 0 g

CHOLESTEROL: 55 mg

SODIUM: 200 mg

POTASSIUM: 243 mg

TOTAL CARBOHYDRATE: 0 g

DIETARY FIBER: 0 g

SUGARS: 0 g

PROTEIN: 18 g

PHOSPHORUS: 156 mg

Pork and Avocado-Lime Wrap

SERVES
1

PREP TIME
10 Minutes

COOK TIME
6 Minutes

SERVING SIZE
About 2 ounces cooked pork, about 1 1/3 cups vegetables, and 1 tortilla

1 (3-ounce) boneless pork loin chop

Black pepper to taste

1 (8-inch) low-carb, high-fiber flour tortilla

1/2 avocado, roughly mashed

1/2 lime, cut in 2 wedges

1 tablespoon chopped fresh cilantro

1 cup shredded romaine lettuce

1 1/2 tablespoons medium picante sauce

1. Coat the pork with cooking spray, and sprinkle with pepper. Heat a small nonstick skillet over medium-high heat. Cook 3–4 minutes or until slightly pink in center. Place on cutting board and thinly slice.

2. Heat tortilla according to package directions. Spoon mashed avocado down center of tortilla, squeeze 1 lime wedge over avocado, top with cilantro, lettuce, pork, and picante sauce. Squeeze remaining lime wedge over all. Fold tortilla to overlap slightly. Cut in half, if desired.

COOK'S NOTE: To prevent the remaining avocado half from discoloring, place the avocado half in a bowl, squeeze with lemon or lime juice, cover with plastic wrap, and refrigerate overnight.

CHOICES/ EXCHANGES
1 Starch, 1 Nonstarchy Vegetable, 3 Lean Protein, 1 1/2 Fat

CALORIES: 290
CALORIES FROM FAT: 140
TOTAL FAT: 15 g
SATURATED FAT: 2 g
TRANS FAT: 0 g

CHOLESTEROL: 50 mg
SODIUM: 470 mg
POTASSIUM: 807 mg
TOTAL CARBOHYDRATE: 20 g
DIETARY FIBER: 13 g

SUGARS: 2 g
PROTEIN: 27 g
PHOSPHORUS: 241 mg

Ham, Pepper, and Pineapple Broiler Packet

SERVES
1

PREP TIME
10 Minutes

COOK TIME
7 Minutes

SERVING SIZE
1 1/2 cups

1 ounce extra-lean diced ham

3/4 cup chopped green bell pepper

3/4 cup frozen pineapple cubes, thawed

2 teaspoons canola oil

1/2 cup pre-cooked whole-grain rice, such as Ready Rice

2 tablespoons water

2 tablespoons chopped green onion

1/16 teaspoon garlic salt (pinch)

1. Preheat broiler.

2. Place the ham, peppers, and pineapple on a baking sheet covered in foil. Drizzle with oil and toss until well coated.

3. Arrange in a single layer and broil 3 minutes. Stir and broil another 3 minutes or until beginning to brown on edges.

4. Add the remaining ingredients, except the garlic salt, to the ham mixture on the foil. Stir until well blended; fold the foil over and seal edges. Broil 1 minute to heat rice. Open packet and sprinkle with garlic salt.

COOK'S NOTE: To thaw frozen pineapple quickly, place pineapple in a microwave-safe bowl. Cover and microwave on high for 30–45 seconds.

CHOICES/ EXCHANGES
1 1/2 Starch, 1 Fruit, 1 Nonstarchy Vegetable, 1 Lean Protein, 2 Fat

CALORIES: 330
CALORIES FROM FAT: 110
TOTAL FAT: 12 g
SATURATED FAT: 1 g
TRANS FAT: 0 g

CHOLESTEROL: 10 mg
SODIUM: 430 mg
POTASSIUM: 384 mg
TOTAL CARBOHYDRATE: 44 g
DIETARY FIBER: 5g

SUGARS: 6 g
PROTEIN: 10 g
PHOSPHORUS: 86 mg

Hash Brown Potatoes with Ham

SERVES	PREP TIME	COOK TIME	STAND TIME
1	10 Minutes	9 Minutes	5 Minutes

SERVING SIZE
About 1 1/4 cups

2 teaspoons canola oil

3/4 cup chopped red bell pepper

1/2 cup chopped onion

4 ounces frozen shredded hash brown potatoes

1 ounce extra-lean ham (96% fat free), diced

1/8 teaspoon dried thyme

1/16 teaspoon garlic salt (pinch)

1 tablespoon light sour cream

Black pepper to taste

1. Heat oil in a medium nonstick skillet over medium heat. Stir in the peppers, onions, potatoes, ham, and thyme. Cook 9 minutes or until potatoes are browned, stirring occasionally.

2. Remove from heat, and sprinkle with the garlic salt. Cover and let stand 5 minutes to absorb flavors and for peak texture. Serve topped with sour cream and black pepper.

CHOICES/ EXCHANGES
1 1/2 Starch, 2 Nonstarchy Vegetable, 1 Lean Protein, 1 1/2 Fat

CALORIES: 290
CALORIES FROM FAT: 110
TOTAL FAT: 13 g
SATURATED FAT: 2 g
TRANS FAT: 0 g

CHOLESTEROL: 15 mg
SODIUM: 460 mg
POTASSIUM: 779 mg
TOTAL CARBOHYDRATE: 36 g
DIETARY FIBER: 5 g

SUGARS: 9 g
PROTEIN: 10 g
PHOSPHORUS: 169 mg

MEATLESS MAINS

Santa Fe Romaine Salad

SERVES
1

PREP TIME
10 Minutes

SERVING SIZE
3 cups

2 cups shredded romaine lettuce

2 tablespoons medium picante sauce

1 tablespoon water

3 tablespoons light sour cream

1 ounce corn tortilla chips, coarsely crumbled ▮

1/4 cup no-salt-added black beans, rinsed and drained ▮▮

2 tablespoons roasted, salted, and hulled pumpkin seeds

2 tablespoons chopped fresh cilantro, optional

1/2 lime, cut in two wedges

1. Place the lettuce on a dinner plate. Stir together the picante sauce and water; spoon over lettuce and top with the remaining ingredients, except lime wedges. Serve with lime wedges.

COOK'S NOTE: Buy snack sizes of corn tortilla chips. They stay fresher longer and are perfect for portion control! You can also divide larger bags of chips into 1-ounce portions and store in snack baggies.

COOK'S NOTE: Place leftover black beans in a freezer sandwich bag and lay flat in the freezer. They will thaw more quickly, and you can also break off the amount you need rather than thawing the entire amount unnecessarily.

CHOICES/ EXCHANGES

2 Starch, 1/2 Carbohydrate, 1 Nonstarchy Vegetable, 1 Lean Protein, 2 1/2 Fat

CALORIES: 360
CALORIES FROM FAT: 150
TOTAL FAT: 17 g
SATURATED FAT: 4.5 g
TRANS FAT: 0 g

CHOLESTEROL: 15 mg
SODIUM: 470 mg
POTASSIUM: 619 mg
TOTAL CARBOHYDRATE: 45 g
DIETARY FIBER: 8 g

SUGARS: 7 g
PROTEIN: 13 g
PHOSPHORUS: 326 mg

Powerhouse Kale Salad

SERVES
1

PREP TIME
10 Minutes

SERVING SIZE
4 cups

3 cups baby kale and greens, such as Dole Power Up Greens

1 hard-boiled egg, peeled and chopped

1/2 cup grape tomatoes, halved

1/2 cup sliced cucumber

1/4 cup chopped red onion

1 1/2 tablespoons cider vinegar

1 tablespoon canola oil

2 teaspoons capers

1/2 teaspoon dried oregano

1/16 teaspoon salt (pinch)

1 (0.67-ounce) slice reduced-fat Swiss cheese, torn into small pieces

1. Combine all ingredients in a medium bowl and toss until well coated.

COOK'S NOTE: You can buy packages of hard-boiled eggs in most supermarkets. They can be found in the deli and/or dairy aisle.

CHOICES/ EXCHANGES
2 Nonstarchy Vegetable, 2 Medium Fat Protein, 2 1/2 Fat

CALORIES: 320
CALORIES FROM FAT: 200
TOTAL FAT: 23 g
SATURATED FAT: 5 g
TRANS FAT: 0 g

CHOLESTEROL: 200 mg
SODIUM: 440 mg
POTASSIUM: 819 mg
TOTAL CARBOHYDRATE: 13 g
DIETARY FIBER: 5 g

SUGARS: 5 g
PROTEIN: 17 g
PHOSPHORUS: 143 mg

Spicy Basil Tomato Pasta with Feta

SERVES
1

PREP TIME
10 Minutes

COOK TIME
10 Minutes

SERVING SIZE
1 cup pasta plus 3/4 cup topping

2 ounces whole-grain spaghetti, such as Barilla Plus, broken in half

1/2 cup grape tomatoes, halved

2 tablespoons chopped fresh basil

2 teaspoons extra-virgin olive oil

1 teaspoon apple cider vinegar

1/2 teaspoon hot sauce, such as Frank's

1/8 teaspoon garlic powder

3 tablespoons crumbled reduced-fat feta cheese

1. Cook pasta according to package directions.

2. Meanwhile, combine remaining ingredients, except the cheese, in a bowl.

3. Drain pasta, place on dinner plate, top with tomato mixture, and sprinkle with cheese.

COOK'S NOTE: Breaking the pasta in half not only makes it easier to eat, but it makes for smaller bites, which give the feeling of eating more!

CHOICES/ EXCHANGES
2 1/2 Starch, 1 Nonstarchy Vegetable, 1 Medium Fat Protein, 1 Fat

CALORIES: 330
CALORIES FROM FAT: 130
TOTAL FAT: 14 g
SATURATED FAT: 3.5 g
TRANS FAT: 0 g

CHOLESTEROL: 10 mg
SODIUM: 440 mg
POTASSIUM: 197 mg
TOTAL CARBOHYDRATE: 43 g
DIETARY FIBER: 6 g

SUGARS: 4 g
PROTEIN: 15 g
PHOSPHORUS: 21 mg

Creamy Rotini with Cauliflower and Peas

SERVES
1

PREP TIME
10 Minutes

COOK TIME
12 Minutes

SERVING SIZE
1 1/2 cups

2 cups water

1 ounce whole-grain rotini, such as Barilla Plus

1 cup frozen cauliflower florets, preferrably smaller florets

1/4 cup frozen green peas

1 ounce reduced-fat cream cheese, cut into small cubes

2 tablespoons shredded reduced-fat sharp cheddar cheese

1/4 teaspoon yellow mustard

1/16 teaspoon salt (pinch)

2 tablespoons finely chopped green onion, optional

1. Bring water to a boil in a medium saucepan. Stir in the rotini and cook 8 minutes. Stir in the frozen cauliflower, reduce heat to medium-high, cover, and cook 4 minutes or until cauliflower is tender-crisp.

2. Remove from heat. Place the frozen peas in a colander, and drain rotini mixture over the peas. Shake off excess liquid.

3. Return to the pot, add remaining ingredients, except green onion, and stir until cheese melts. Sprinkle with onion, if desired.

COOK'S NOTE: For a thinner consistency, stir in 1 tablespoon water.

CHOICES/ EXCHANGES
1 1/2 Starch,
1 Nonstarchy Vegetable,
1 Medium Fat Protein,
1/2 Fat

CALORIES: 250
CALORIES FROM FAT: 70
TOTAL FAT: 8 g
SATURATED FAT: 4.5 g
TRANS FAT: 0 g

CHOLESTEROL: 25 mg
SODIUM: 480 mg
POTASSIUM: 265 mg
TOTAL CARBOHYDRATE: 31 g
DIETARY FIBER: 7 g

SUGARS: 5 g
PROTEIN: 13 g
PHOSPHORUS: 550 mg

Fast Fix Fried Rice

SERVES
1

PREP TIME
10 Minutes

COOK TIME
6 Minutes

SERVING SIZE
About 1 1/3 cups

2 teaspoons light butter with canola oil

1 teaspoon canola oil

1/2 cup cooked brown rice

2 tablespoons slivered almonds

1 egg, beaten

1/4 cup chopped green onions

1/4 cup frozen peas

1 1/2 teaspoons light soy sauce

1. Melt light butter with the oil in a medium nonstick skillet over medium heat. Cook rice and almonds 4 minutes or until rice is lightly browned, stirring constantly.

2. Working quickly, stir in the remaining ingredients, except the soy sauce. Cook, stirring constantly, 30 seconds or until egg is cooked, breaking up any large pieces. Remove from heat and sprinkle with soy sauce.

COOK'S NOTE: This is a great way to use leftover rice, but if you don't have any on hand, use the frozen whole-grain rice or a pouch of whole-grain rice, such as Ready Rice (unseasoned variety). Freeze remaining rice for later use. May want to freeze the pouch variety in 1/2 cup portions—for portion control.

CHOICES/ EXCHANGES
2 Starch, 1/2 Carbohydrate,
1 Medium Fat Protein,
3 Fat

CALORIES: 400
CALORIES FROM FAT: 200
TOTAL FAT: 22 g
SATURATED FAT: 4 g
TRANS FAT: 0 g

CHOLESTEROL: 190 mg
SODIUM: 470 mg
POTASSIUM: 338 mg
TOTAL CARBOHYDRATE: 33 g
DIETARY FIBER: 6 g

SUGARS: 4 g
PROTEIN: 15 g
PHOSPHORUS: 297 mg

DESIGNED FOR ONE!

High-Roasted Potato and Veggie Packet

SERVES
1

PREP TIME
10 Minutes

COOK TIME
10 Minutes

STAND TIME
3 Minutes

SERVING SIZE
2 cups

6 ounces red potato, cut into 1/2-inch cubes

1/2 cup chopped onion

1 cup chopped green bell pepper

2 teaspoons canola oil

1/8 teaspoon dried thyme

1/8 teaspoon salt

3 tablespoons shredded reduced-fat sharp cheddar cheese

1. Preheat broiler.

2. Place potatoes, onion, and peppers on a foil-lined baking sheet, and drizzle with oil and toss until well coated. Arrange in a single layer and broil 5 minutes. Stir and broil 4 minutes or until vegetables are tender and beginning to brown.

3. Remove from broiler, and sprinkle with thyme. Stir and pull up the ends of the foil, and twist ends to seal. Let stand 3 minutes to allow flavors to absorb and natural juices to be released. Roll back the foil and sprinkle with the salt and cheese.

> **COOK'S NOTE:** It's important to cut the potato into 1/2-inch pieces for quick and even cooking. An easy way to do this is to first cut the potato into 1/2-inch-thick slices, and then cut each slice into 1/2-inch cubes.

CHOICES/ EXCHANGES
2 Starch, 2 Nonstarchy Vegetable, 1 Medium Fat Protein, 1 Fat

CALORIES: 330
CALORIES FROM FAT: 130
TOTAL FAT: 14 g
SATURATED FAT: 3.5 g
TRANS FAT: 0 g

CHOLESTEROL: 15 mg
SODIUM: 460 mg
POTASSIUM: 1165 mg
TOTAL CARBOHYDRATE: 42 g
DIETARY FIBER: 7 g

SUGARS: 9 g
PROTEIN: 11 g
PHOSPHORUS: 267 mg

Corn and Green Pepper Frittata

SERVES
1

PREP TIME
10 Minutes

COOK TIME
5 Minutes

SERVING SIZE
1 frittata

1 cup frozen corn kernels, thawed

1/3 cup finely chopped green onion

3 tablespoons finely chopped green bell pepper 🔳

1 large egg

1 tablespoon water

1/16 teaspoon ground cumin, optional (pinch)

2 tablespoons grated reduced-fat Mexican blend cheese

1/8 teaspoon salt

1. Heat a small nonstick skillet coated with cooking spray over medium-low heat. Add the corn, onion, and bell pepper. Stir to blend, cover, and cook 2 minutes or until heated through.

2. Whisk together the egg, water, and cumin; pour over all. Cover and cook 2 minutes or until eggs are set.

3. Remove from heat, and sprinkle evenly with the cheese and salt. Let stand, uncovered, for 1 minute. Gently remove from the skillet by sliding a rubber spatula around and under the egg mixture and then sliding onto a dinner plate.

🔳 **COOK'S NOTE:** For a spicier dish, replace the bell pepper with a large jalapeño, seeded and membranes removed.

CHOICES/ EXCHANGES
2 Starch, 1 Nonstarchy Vegetable, 1 Medium Fat Protein

CALORIES: 250
CALORIES FROM FAT: 80
TOTAL FAT: 9 g
SATURATED FAT: 3.5 g
TRANS FAT: 0 g

CHOLESTEROL: 195 mg
SODIUM: 470 mg
POTASSIUM: 501 mg
TOTAL CARBOHYDRATE: 33 g
DIETARY FIBER: 5 g

SUGARS: 6 g
PROTEIN: 15 g
PHOSPHORUS: 200 mg

Feta and Basil Omelet

SERVES
1

PREP TIME
10 Minutes

COOK TIME
3 Minutes

SERVING SIZE
1 omelet plus 1/2 cup vegetables

2 large eggs

2 tablespoons chopped fresh basil, divided use

2 tablespoons water

1 teaspoon canola oil

1/2 cup grape tomatoes, quartered

3 tablespoons crumbled reduced-fat feta cheese

2 tablespoons finely chopped green onion

Black pepper to taste

1. In a bowl, whisk together eggs, 1 tablespoon basil, and water until smooth.

2. Heat the oil in a medium nonstick skillet over medium-high heat. Add the egg mixture and cook 1 minute without stirring. Using a rubber spatula, lift up edges to allow uncooked portion to run under. Cook 1–2 minutes longer or until almost set and beginning to puff up slightly. (You may want to run the spatula gently over the surface to spread any uncooked portion around.)

3. Sprinkle the remaining ingredients down one side of the omelet and gently fold over.

4. Place on dinner plate, and sprinkle with additional black pepper, if desired.

CHOICES/ EXCHANGES

1 Nonstarchy Vegetable, 2 Medium Fat Protein, 1 1/2 Fat

CALORIES: 250
CALORIES FROM FAT: 160
TOTAL FAT: 17 g
SATURATED FAT: 5 g
TRANS FAT: 0 g

CHOLESTEROL: 380 mg
SODIUM: 450 mg
POTASSIUM: 397 mg
TOTAL CARBOHYDRATE: 5 g
DIETARY FIBER: 2 g

SUGARS: 3 g
PROTEIN: 18 g
PHOSPHORUS: 221 mg

Arugula Mozzarella Tortilla Flat

SERVES
1

PREP TIME
5 Minutes

COOK TIME
3 Minutes

SERVING SIZE
1 tortilla

1 (8-inch) low-carb, high-fiber flour tortilla

1/8 teaspoon garlic powder

1/16 teaspoon crushed pepper flakes (pinch)

1 tablespoon chopped fresh basil

3 tablespoons shredded part-skim mozzarella cheese

3/4 cup arugula

1 teaspoon extra-virgin olive oil

1 teaspoon cider vinegar

1 teaspoon grated Parmesan cheese

1. Heat a medium nonstick skillet over medium-low heat. Coat both sides of the tortilla with cooking spray. Cook tortilla 1 minute, turn, top with the garlic powder, pepper flakes, basil, and mozzarella cheese. Cook 1 minute or until cheese melts.

2. Meanwhile, combine the arugula, oil, and vinegar in a bowl and toss until well coated.

3. Remove tortilla from skillet, and cut into 4 wedges. Top each wedge with a small mound of the arugula mixture and sprinkle evenly with the cheese.

COOK'S NOTE: You can use scissors to cut the tortilla into wedges.

CHOICES/ EXCHANGES

1 Starch, 1 Medium Fat Protein, 1 Fat

CALORIES: 200

CALORIES FROM FAT: 110

TOTAL FAT: 12 g

SATURATED FAT: 5 g

TRANS FAT: 0 g

CHOLESTEROL: 15 mg

SODIUM: 480 mg

POTASSIUM: 89 mg

TOTAL CARBOHYDRATE: 13 g

DIETARY FIBER: 6 g

SUGARS: 1 g

PROTEIN: 12 g

PHOSPHORUS: 2 g

Red Pepper–Mushroom Skillet Pizza

SERVES 1
PREP TIME 10 Minutes
COOK TIME 7 Minutes
SERVING SIZE 1 tortilla plus about 1 cup vegetables

1 (8-inch) low-carb, high-fiber flour tortilla

2 tablespoons low-sodium marinara sauce, such as Prego Heart Smart

1 tablespoon chopped fresh basil, or 1 teaspoon dried basil

2 ounces sliced mushrooms

1/3 cup chopped red bell pepper

1 ounce shredded part-skim mozzarella cheese

1/16 teaspoon dried pepper flakes (pinch)

1 teaspoon grated Parmesan cheese

1. Coat both sides of the tortilla with cooking spray. Place in a medium nonstick skillet. Spread spaghetti sauce evenly over tortilla. Top with the remaining ingredients, except the Parmesan cheese.

2. Place over low heat, cover, and cook 7 minutes or until lightly browned on bottom and cheese has melted. Remove from heat and sprinkle with Parmesan cheese.

COOK'S NOTE: Store remaining mushrooms in a paper lunch bag in the crisper for up to 4 days. It's a great "free" veggie to add to your favorite salad, soup, or sandwich, too.

CHOICES/ EXCHANGES
1 Starch, 1 Nonstarchy Vegetable, 1 Medium Fat Protein, 1/2 Fat

CALORIES: 190
CALORIES FROM FAT: 90
TOTAL FAT: 10 g
SATURATED FAT: 4 g
TRANS FAT: 0 g

CHOLESTEROL: 20 mg
SODIUM: 480 mg
POTASSIUM: 400 mg
TOTAL CARBOHYDRATE: 19 g
DIETARY FIBER: 9 g

SUGARS: 5 g
PROTEIN: 16 g
PHOSPHORUS: 80 mg

TWO-FOR-ONE

Chicken with Artichoke-Blue Cheese Topping

SERVES
2

PREP TIME
5 Minutes

COOK TIME
6 Minutes

SERVING SIZE
3 1/4 ounces cooked chicken plus 3/4 cup artichoke mixture

6 chicken tenderloins (about 9 ounces total)

1 1/2 tablespoons extra-virgin olive oil, divided use

1/4 teaspoon black pepper

1/2 (9-ounce) package quartered artichoke hearts

1 teaspoon grated lemon zest

1 tablespoon fresh lemon juice

6 pitted kalamata olives, coarsely chopped

3 tablespoons crumbled reduced-fat blue cheese

2 tablespoons chopped fresh parsley

1 garlic clove, minced

1/2 teaspoon dried oregano or rosemary

1. Sprinkle both sides of the chicken with pepper. Heat 1 1/2 teaspoons oil in a medium nonstick skillet over medium-high heat. Cook chicken 3 minutes on each side or until no longer pink in center.

2. Meanwhile, pat dry artichokes on paper towels and combine with 1 tablespoon oil and the remaining ingredients in a bowl; set aside.

3. Divide chicken into 2 servings. Top with artichoke mixture. You can serve half and reserve half of the chicken and half of the artichoke mixture (preferably stored separately) for Chicken, Artichoke, and Green Bean Salad (page 115).

COOK'S NOTE: Thaw artichokes by placing in a microwave-safe bowl, cover, and microwave on high for 2–3 minutes. May refrigerate unused portion for salads up to 3 days or return to freezer for a later use.

CHOICES/ EXCHANGES
1 Nonstarchy Vegetable, 5 Lean Protein, 1 1/2 Fat

CALORIES: 310
CALORIES FROM FAT: 150
TOTAL FAT: 17 g
SATURATED FAT: 3 g
TRANS FAT: 0 g

CHOLESTEROL: 70 mg
SODIUM: 430 mg
POTASSIUM: 174 mg
TOTAL CARBOHYDRATE: 7 g
DIETARY FIBER: 3 g

SUGARS: 0 g
PROTEIN: 35 g
PHOSPHORUS: 40 mg

Chicken, Artichoke, and Green Bean Salad

SERVES
1

PREP TIME
5 Minutes

COOK TIME
3 Minutes

SERVING SIZE
About 3 cups

4 ounces green beans, broken into 2-inch pieces (1 cup)

1 cup water

Reserved Chicken with Artichoke-Blue Cheese Topping (page 114)

1/4 cup chopped red onion

2 tablespoons white (or golden) balsamic vinegar

1/2 teaspoon sugar

1/16 teaspoon crushed pepper flakes (pinch)

1 cup spring greens or arugula

1. Combine the beans and water in a small saucepan. Bring to a boil, reduce heat, cover, and simmer 3 minutes or until beans are just tender-crisp. Drain and run under cold water to cool quickly and stop cooking process. Drain well.

2. Chop the reserve chicken and place in a bowl with the beans and remaining ingredients. Toss until well blended.

COOK'S NOTE: White balsamic vinegar (sometimes labeled "golden" balsamic vinegar) is a lighter, sweeter version of the traditional balsamic variety. It's lighter in color and taste and has faint "vanilla-like" characteristics—a terrific addition to your staples!

CHOICES/ EXCHANGES
1/2 Carbohydrate,
3 Nonstarchy Vegetable,
5 Lean Protein,
1 1/2 Fat

CALORIES: 370
CALORIES FROM FAT: 150
TOTAL FAT: 17 g
SATURATED FAT: 3 g
TRANS FAT: 0 g

CHOLESTEROL: 70 mg
SODIUM: 480 mg
POTASSIUM: 447 mg
TOTAL CARBOHYDRATE: 22 g
DIETARY FIBER: 8 g

SUGARS: 9 g
PROTEIN: 37 g
PHOSPHORUS: 40 mg

Chicken-Spinach Couscous

SERVES
2

PREP TIME
10 Minutes

COOK TIME
11 Minutes

SERVING SIZE
1 1/2 cups couscous mixture

8 ounces boneless, skinless chicken breast, cut into bite-size pieces

1/2 cup chopped onion

1 teaspoon dried oregano

2/3 cup water

1/2 cup whole-wheat pearl couscous

2 cups fresh baby spinach, coarsely chopped

1/8 teaspoon garlic salt

2 or 4 tablespoons grated Parmesan cheese

1. Heat a medium nonstick skillet over medium-high heat, and coat the chicken with cooking spray and cook 1 minute. Do not stir. Stir in the onions and oregano, cook 2 minutes, and add the water and couscous. Bring to a boil over medium-high heat. Reduce heat, cover, and simmer 8 minutes or until couscous is tender and liquid is absorbed.

2. Reduce heat to medium-low, and stir the spinach and garlic salt into the couscous mixture until spinach is slightly wilted.

3. Divide into 2 servings, if desired. Sprinkle the half that is being served immediately with 2 tablespoons Parmesan cheese. If serving 2, sprinkle all with 4 tablespoons cheese. You can serve half and reserve half of the couscous mixture for Pepperoncini Chicken Couscous Salad (page 117).

CHOICES/ EXCHANGES
2 1/2 Starch,
1 Nonstarchy Vegetable,
4 Lean Protein

CALORIES: 400
CALORIES FROM FAT: 70
TOTAL FAT: 8 g
SATURATED FAT: 3.5 g
TRANS FAT: 0 g

CHOLESTEROL: 100 mg
SODIUM: 410 mg
POTASSIUM: 437 mg
TOTAL CARBOHYDRATE: 43 g
DIETARY FIBER: 8 g

SUGARS: 3 g
PROTEIN: 40 g
PHOSPHORUS: 253 mg

Pepperoncini Chicken Couscous Salad

SERVES
1

PREP TIME
5 Minutes

SERVING SIZE
2 cups

Reserved Chicken-Spinach
Couscous (page 116)

1/4 cup grape tomatoes,
quartered (or 1 small plum
tomato, chopped)

3/4 ounce sliced pepperoncini
peppers (about 3 tablespoons)

1 teaspoon dried dill

1 teaspoon extra-virgin olive oil

1 to 1 1/2 teaspoons cider
vinegar

1. Combine all ingredients. Toss until well blended.

**CHOICES/
EXCHANGES**
2 1/2 Starch,
2 Nonstarchy Vegetable,
3 Lean Protein, 1/2 Fat

CALORIES: 390
CALORIES FROM FAT: 80
TOTAL FAT: 8 g
SATURATED FAT: 1.5 g
TRANS FAT: 0 g

CHOLESTEROL: 85 mg
SODIUM: 430 mg
POTASSIUM: 525 mg
TOTAL CARBOHYDRATE: 45 g
DIETARY FIBER: 9 g

SUGARS: 4 g
PROTEIN: 35 g
PHOSPHORUS: 262 mg

Sausage and Potato Stuffed Portobellos

SERVES
2

PREP TIME
10 Minutes

COOK TIME
20 Minutes

STAND TIME
5 Minutes

SERVING SIZE
2 mushroom caps, about 1 cup potato mixture, and 1/2 ounce cheese

3/4 cup turkey sausage crumbles, such as Jimmy Dean

1 tablespoon canola oil

8 ounces frozen shredded hash browns

3/4 cup chopped onion

1/4 teaspoon dried Italian seasoning

1/8 teaspoon crushed pepper flakes, optional

1/8 teaspoon garlic salt

4 portobello mushroom caps, about 12 ounces total

1 ounce shredded reduced-fat sharp cheddar cheese

2 tablespoons chopped fresh parsley, optional

1. Preheat broiler.

2. Heat a medium nonstick skillet over medium-high heat. Lightly coat sausage with cooking spray and cook 2 minutes or until beginning to brown. Set aside.

3. Reduce heat to medium, heat the oil. Add the potatoes, onions, Italian seasoning, and pepper flakes; cook 9 minutes or until potatoes are beginning to lightly brown, stirring occasionally.

4. Stir the sausage and garlic salt into the potato mixture. Remove from heat, cover, and let stand 5 minutes to absorb flavors and for peak texture.

5. Meanwhile, coat both sides of the mushroom caps with cooking spray; place on a foil-lined baking sheet coated with cooking spray. Broil 3 minutes on each side or until mushrooms are tender.

6. Spoon equal amounts of the sausage mixture on top of each mushroom cap (about 1/2 cup per cap), sprinkle evenly with the cheese. You can serve half of the stuffed mushrooms and reserve half for Portobello, Potato, and Sausage Egg Skillet (page 119).

CHOICES/ EXCHANGES
1 1/2 Starch,
2 Nonstarchy Vegetable,
1 Lean Protein, 2 Fat

CALORIES: 300
CALORIES FROM FAT: 110
TOTAL FAT: 13 g
SATURATED FAT: 3 g
TRANS FAT: 0 g

CHOLESTEROL: 20 mg
SODIUM: 400 mg
POTASSIUM: 1390 mg
TOTAL CARBOHYDRATE: 33 g
DIETARY FIBER: 5 g

SUGARS: 7 g
PROTEIN: 17 g
PHOSPHORUS: 435 mg

Portobello, Potato, and Sausage Egg Skillet

SERVES
1

PREP TIME
5 Minutes

COOK TIME
5 Minutes

SERVING SIZE
2 cups mushroom mixture and 1 egg

Reserved Sausage and Potato
    Stuffed Portobellos
    (page 118)
1/2 teaspoon canola oil
1 large egg

1. Chop the stuffed mushrooms and place on a microwave-safe dinner plate or in a shallow bowl with the reserved potato mixture and cheese. Cover and microwave on high for 2 minutes or until thoroughly heated.

2. Meanwhile, heat the oil in a small nonstick skillet over over medium heat. Tilt skillet to coat bottom lightly. Crack egg into the skillet and cook 3 minutes or until egg white is opaque. Do NOT stir or turn over. Sprinkle with black pepper and serve over mushroom mixture.

**CHOICES/
EXCHANGES**
1 1/2 Starch,
2 Nonstarchy Vegetable,
2 Lean Protein,
2 1/2 Fat

CALORIES: 370
CALORIES FROM FAT: 160
TOTAL FAT: 18 g
SATURATED FAT: 4.5 g
TRANS FAT: 0 g

CHOLESTEROL: 210 mg
SODIUM: 470 mg
POTASSIUM: 1460 mg
TOTAL CARBOHYDRATE: 33 g
DIETARY FIBER: 5 g

SUGARS: 8 g
PROTEIN: 23 g
PHOSPHORUS: 530 mg

Garden Fresh Vegetable Pasta Toss

SERVES
2

PREP TIME
10 Minutes

COOK TIME
10 Minutes

SERVING SIZE
2 cups

3 cups water

4 ounces whole-grain rotini, such as Barilla Plus

1 1/2 cups fresh baby spinach

3/4 cup grape tomatoes, halved

1/4 cup chopped fresh basil

1/4 teaspoon dried rosemary

1 jalapeño pepper, seeded and finely chopped

1 tablespoon extra-virgin olive oil

1/2 teaspoon garlic salt

2 tablespoons grated Parmesan cheese

1. Bring the water to a boil in a medium saucepan, add the noodles, and cook 10 minutes or until tender. Drain, reserving 1/4 cup pasta water.

2. Place the cooked pasta and pasta water in a medium bowl with the remaining ingredients, except the Parmesan cheese. Toss until spinach is slightly wilted. Sprinkle with the Parmesan cheese.

3. Divide into 2 servings. You can serve half and reserve half of the pasta mixture for Petite Pepper Pasta Salad (page 121).

CHOICES/ EXCHANGES
2 1/2 Starch, 1 Nonstarchy Vegetable, 1 Lean Protein, 1 1/2 Fat

CALORIES: 320
CALORIES FROM FAT: 100
TOTAL FAT: 11 g
SATURATED FAT: 2.5 g
TRANS FAT: 0 g

CHOLESTEROL: 10 mg
SODIUM: 410 mg
POTASSIUM: 570 mg
TOTAL CARBOHYDRATE: 41 g
DIETARY FIBER: 5 g

SUGARS: 4 g
PROTEIN: 14 g
PHOSPHORUS: 230 mg

Petite Pepper Pasta Salad

SERVES
1

PREP TIME
5 Minutes

SERVING SIZE
3 cups

Reserved Garden Fresh
   Vegetable Pasta Toss
   (page 120)

3 ounces petite peppers,
   stemmed and sliced
   crosswise (to make rings)

1 1/2 tablespoons cider vinegar

1 teaspoon extra-virgin olive oil

1/8 teaspoon lemon pepper
   seasoning

1. Combine all ingredients; toss until well blended.

**CHOICES/
EXCHANGES**
2 1/2 Starch,
2 Nonstarchy Vegetable,
1 Lean Protein,
2 1/2 Fat

CALORIES: 380
CALORIES FROM FAT: 150
TOTAL FAT: 16 g
SATURATED FAT: 3 g
TRANS FAT: 0 g

CHOLESTEROL: 10 mg
SODIUM: 450 mg
POTASSIUM: 750 mg
TOTAL CARBOHYDRATE: 45 g
DIETARY FIBER: 6 g

SUGARS: 6 g
PROTEIN: 15 g
PHOSPHORUS: 250 mg

Slow-Cooker Chuck and Veggies

SERVES
2

PREP TIME
15 Minutes

COOK TIME
4 1/2 hours on high or 9 hours on low

SERVING SIZE
1 1/2 cups beef and veggie mixture

8 ounces boneless lean chuck roast

8 ounces frozen pepper stir-fry

8 ounces whole mushrooms

5 ounces green beans, trimmed (about 1 1/4 cups total)

1/4 cup dry red wine

1 dried bay leaf

1 teaspoon instant coffee granules

1 teaspoon Worcestershire sauce

1/4 teaspoon black pepper

1/4 teaspoon salt

1. Combine all ingredients, except the salt, in a 3 1/2–4-quart slow cooker. Cover and cook on high setting for 4 1/2 hours or on low setting for 9 hours or until beef is very tender. Gently stir in the salt.

2. Remove the beef and vegetables with a slotted spoon and place in 2 shallow bowls.

3. Pour the liquid in the slow cooker into a medium skillet. Bring to a boil over medium-high heat and cook 1 1/2 minutes or until the liquid reduces to 1/4 cup. Spoon evenly over the beef and vegetables. Remove bay leaf before serving. You can serve half and reserve half of the beef and vegetable mixture for Saucy Beef and Egg Noodles (page 123).

COOK'S NOTE: When buying chuck, even when it is labeled "lean," there may still be some fat that needs to be removed. If a butcher is not available to cut a chuck roast to your specifications (lean and 8 ounces), buy a larger piece, trim the fat, and cut it into 8-ounce portions to freeze for later uses.

CHOICES/ EXCHANGES
3 Nonstarchy Vegetable, 3 Lean Protein

CALORIES: 215
CALORIES FROM FAT: 45
TOTAL FAT: 5 g
SATURATED FAT: 1.5 g
TRANS FAT: 0 g

CHOLESTEROL: 45 mg
SODIUM: 380 mg
POTASSIUM: 910 mg
TOTAL CARBOHYDRATE: 17 g
DIETARY FIBER: 5 g

SUGARS: 9 g
PROTEIN: 26 g
PHOSPHORUS: 335 mg

Powerhouse Kale Salad
page 103

Raspberry Orange Spring Salad
page 23

Red Pepper-Mushroom Skillet Pizza
page 111

Sweet Tart Raspberry Phyllo Bites
page 134

Sirloin Strips with Blue Cheese Rotini
page 90

Mediterranean Unstuffed Peppers
page 91

Slow-Cooker Chuck and Veggies
page 122

Tuna Steak with Sweet Pepper-Ginger Relish
page 82

Saucy Beef and Egg Noodles

SERVES	PREP TIME	COOK TIME
1	10 Minutes	13 Minutes

SERVING SIZE
1 1/2 cups beef mixture plus about 3/4 cup noodles

2 cups water

1 ounce yolk-free egg noodles

Reserved Slow-Cooker Chuck and
  Veggies (page 122)

3 tablespoons frozen green peas

1 teaspoon ketchup

1/4 teaspoon Worcestershire
  sauce

1 tablespoon chopped fresh
  parsley, optional

1. Bring the water to a boil in a medium saucepan, add the noodles, and cook 10 minutes or until tender. Drain well.

2. Meanwhile, place the beef mixture and peas in a medium saucepan over medium heat. Cook 2–3 minutes or until heated through, breaking up larger pieces of beef.

3. Remove from heat, and stir in the ketchup and Worcestershire sauce. Serve over drained noodles. Sprinkle with parsley, if desired.

**CHOICES/
EXCHANGES**

1 1/2 Starch,
3 Nonstarchy Vegetable,
3 Lean Protein

CALORIES: 370
CALORIES FROM FAT: 50
TOTAL FAT: 5 g
SATURATED FAT: 1.5 g
TRANS FAT: 0 g

CHOLESTEROL: 45 mg
SODIUM: 480 mg
POTASSIUM: 1030 mg
TOTAL CARBOHYDRATE: 42 g
DIETARY FIBER: 7 g

SUGARS: 12 g
PROTEIN: 32 g
PHOSPHORUS: 415 mg

Picante Beef Over Squash

SERVES **PREP TIME** **COOK TIME**
2 5 Minutes 8 Minutes
SERVING SIZE
3/4 cup beef mixture and 2 squash halves

8 ounces 93% lean ground beef

1/3 cup medium picante sauce

1 teaspoon ground cumin

3/4 teaspoon sugar

2 crookneck squash, (about 12 ounces total), cut in half lengthwise

1/8 teaspoon garlic salt

1. Heat a medium nonstick skillet over medium-high heat. Add the beef and cook 2–3 minutes or until beef is browned. Stir in picante, cumin, and sugar; cook 1 minute.

2. Meanwhile, place squash halves, cut side up, on a microwave-safe plate. Cover and cook on high for 5 minutes or until just tender. Spoon beef mixture evenly over the squash.

3. Divide into 2 servings. You can serve half and reserve half of the beef mixture and half of the squash for Cumin Beef and Squash Bowl (page 125).

**CHOICES/
EXCHANGES**
2 Nonstarchy
Vegetable, 3 Lean
Protein, 1/2 Fat

CALORIES: 220
CALORIES FROM FAT: 80
TOTAL FAT: 8 g
SATURATED FAT: 3.5 g
TRANS FAT: 0 g

CHOLESTEROL: 70 mg
SODIUM: 440 mg
POTASSIUM: 378 mg
TOTAL CARBOHYDRATE: 10 g
DIETARY FIBER: 2 g

SUGARS: 7 g
PROTEIN: 25 g
PHOSPHORUS: 54 mg

Cumin Beef and Squash Bowl

SERVES
1

PREP TIME
5 Minutes

COOK TIME
2 Minutes

SERVING SIZE
1 1/2 cups total

Reserved Picante Beef Over
Squash (page 124)

2 tablespoons chopped fresh
cilantro

1/8 teaspoon ground cumin

1/8 teaspoon hot sauce, such as
Frank's

2 teaspoons light sour cream

1. Chop the reserved squash and place in a microwave-safe bowl with the reserved picante beef mixture, cilantro, cumin, and hot sauce. Cover and microwave on high for 2–3 minutes or until heated through.

2. Top with sour cream.

**CHOICES/
EXCHANGES**
2 Nonstarchy
Vegetable, 3 Lean
Protein, 1 Fat

CALORIES: 230
CALORIES FROM FAT: 90
TOTAL FAT: 10 g
SATURATED FAT: 4 g
TRANS FAT: 0 g

CHOLESTEROL: 75 mg
SODIUM: 480 mg
POTASSIUM: 411 mg
TOTAL CARBOHYDRATE: 11 g
DIETARY FIBER: 2 g

SUGARS: 7 g
PROTEIN: 26 g
PHOSPHORUS: 63 mg

Pork Tenderloin with Roasted Squash

SERVES
2

PREP TIME
10 Minutes

COOK TIME
27 Minutes

STAND TIME
5 Minutes

SERVING SIZE
3 ounces cooked pork and about 1 1/4 cups vegetable mixture

8 ounces pork tenderloin

1 medium onion, cut in
8 wedges (4 ounces)

1 (15-ounce) package frozen
butternut squash cubes

1 tablespoon extra-virgin olive
oil

1 tablespoon mango chutney

1/2 teaspoon garlic salt

1/4 teaspoon dried rosemary

1. Preheat oven to 425°F.

2. Coat the pork with cooking spray, and heat a small nonstick skillet over medium-high heat. Brown pork on all sides, about 4 minutes.

3. Combine the onions and frozen squash on a foil-lined baking sheet coated with cooking spray. Drizzle with oil, toss until well coated, and arrange in a single layer. Place the pork in the center of vegetables and brush the pork with chutney. Bake 22 minutes or until internal temperature of the pork reaches 145°F. Place pork on cutting board and let stand 5 minutes before slicing.

4. Meanwhile, sprinkle the vegetables with the garlic salt and rosemary. Do not stir. Bake 5 minutes or until squash is tender. Gently stir, scraping the foil to release pan drippings, and stir into the vegetable mixture.

5. Divide pork and squash mixture each into 2 servings. You can serve half and reserve half of the pork and half of the vegetables (storing separately) for Roasted Squash Soup with Pork (page 127).

COOK'S NOTE: Your butcher can cut a tenderloin to the weight needed. If the butcher is not available, a larger tenderloin may be purchased. Cut it in half and place the unused portion in the freezer for a later date.

**CHOICES/
EXCHANGES**
2 Starch, 1 Nonstarchy
Vegetable, 3 Lean
Protein, 1/2 Fat

CALORIES: 330
CALORIES FROM FAT: 90
TOTAL FAT: 10 g
SATURATED FAT: 2 g
TRANS FAT: 0 g

CHOLESTEROL: 75 mg
SODIUM: 400 mg
POTASSIUM: 1272 mg
TOTAL CARBOHYDRATE: 36 g
DIETARY FIBER: 5 g

SUGARS: 13 g
PROTEIN: 26 g
PHOSPHORUS: 365 mg

Roasted Squash Soup with Pork

SERVES
1

PREP TIME
10 Minutes

COOK TIME
2 Minutes

SERVING SIZE
1 2/3 cups soup plus 3 ounces cooked pork

Reserved Pork Tenderloin with Roasted Squash (page 126)

2/3 cup fat-free milk

1/16 teaspoon dried rosemary (pinch)

Black pepper to taste

2 tablespoons finely chopped green onion, optional

1. Dice the pork and set aside.

2. Combine the reserved vegetables, milk, and rosemary in a blender, secure with lid and purée until smooth.

3. Pour the puréed mixture into a soup bowl (for a thinner consistency, stir in 1–2 tablespoons water), top with the pork and sprinkle with pepper. Cover and microwave on high for 1–2 minutes or until heated. Sprinkle with green onions, if desired.

**CALORIES/
EXCHANGES**
2 Starch, 1/2 Fat-Free Milk, 1 Nonstarchy Vegetable, 3 Lean Protein, 1/2 Fat

CALORIES: 390
CALORIES FROM FAT: 90
TOTAL FAT: 10 g
SATURATED FAT: 2 g
TRANS FAT: 0 g

CHOLESTEROL: 75 mg
SODIUM: 480 mg
POTASSIUM: 1551 mg
TOTAL CARBOHYDRATE: 44 g
DIETARY FIBER: 5 g

SUGARS: 21 g
PROTEIN: 32 g
PHOSPHORUS: 535 mg

Spiced Pork with Avocado Aioli

SERVES 2

PREP TIME 10 Minutes

COOK TIME 22 Minutes

STAND TIME 3 Minutes

SERVING SIZE
3 ounces cooked pork and 6 tablespoons avocado mixture

8 ounces pork tenderloin

2 teaspoons canola oil

1/2 teaspoon ground cumin

1/4 teaspoon ground allspice

1/16 teaspoon crushed pepper flakes (pinch)

Black pepper to taste

1/8 teaspoon salt, divided use

1 avocado, peeled and sliced

1 tablespoon light sour cream

1 small garlic clove, minced

1 lime, cut in 4 wedges

1. Preheat oven to 425°F.

2. Place pork on a foil-lined baking sheet. Brush the oil over the pork, sprinkle with the cumin, allspice, pepper flakes, and black pepper. Bake 20–22 minutes or until internal temperature reaches 145°F.

3. Place on cutting board and let stand 3 minutes before thinly slicing. Once sliced, sprinkle with 1/16 teaspoon (pinch) of salt.

4. Meanwhile, place the avocado, sour cream, garlic, and remaining salt in a bowl and using a fork, roughly mash.

5. Divide tenderloin and avocado mixture each into 2 servings.

6. Serve remaining pork over a bed of the avocado mixture and squeeze 2 lime wedges over all. You can serve half and reserve half of the pork, half of the avocado mixture , and 2 lime wedges for Pork and Black Bean Salad with Guacamole (page 129).

COOK'S NOTE: If reserving avocado mixture, squeeze a small amount of lime juice evenly over the avocado mixture and seal with plastic wrap. Place the plastic wrap directly on the surface of the avocado mixture to prevent discoloration. If the mixture does discolor slightly, it is still good; just stir the mixture before serving.

CHOICES/ EXCHANGES
1/2 Carbohydrate,
3 Lean Protein, 2 Fat

CALORIES: 250
CALORIES FROM FAT: 120
TOTAL FAT: 14 g
SATURATED FAT: 3 g
TRANS FAT: 0 g

CHOLESTEROL: 75 mg
SODIUM: 220 mg
POTASSIUM: 838 mg
TOTAL CARBOHYDRATE: 8 g
DIETARY FIBER: 5 g

SUGARS: 0 g
PROTEIN: 26 g
PHOSPHORUS: 327 mg

Pork and Black Bean Salad with Guacamole

SERVES
1

PREP TIME
10 Minutes

SERVING SIZE
1 1/2 cups pork mixture, 6 tablespoons guacamole, and about 1/3 cup tomatoes

Reserved Spiced Pork with Avocado Aioli (page 128) and 2 lime wedges

1/2 cup no-salt-added black or kidney beans, rinsed and drained

2 tablespoons chopped red onion

2 tablespoons fresh cilantro

1 thinly sliced plum tomato

1/16 teaspoon salt (pinch)

1. Chop the pork and toss with the beans, onion, and cilantro.

2. Place the tomato slices on a dinner plate. Spoon the avocado mixture on top of the tomatoes. Spoon the pork mixture over the avocado mixture, squeeze lime over, and sprinkle with the salt.

COOK'S NOTE: Freeze leftover canned beans by placing them in a resealable sandwich baggie, sealing tightly, and freeze them flat in a thin layer. By doing so, it's easy to break off what you need after they are frozen or you can run under cold water to release the amount you need and continue freezing any unused portion.

**CHOICES/
EXCHANGES**
1 Starch, 1/2 Carbohydrate,
1 Nonstarchy Vegetable,
4 Lean Protein, 1 Fat

CALORIES: 370
CALORIES FROM FAT: 130
TOTAL FAT: 14 g
SATURATED FAT: 3 g
TRANS FAT: 0 g

CHOLESTEROL: 75 mg
SODIUM: 380 mg
POTASSIUM: 1304 mg
TOTAL CARBOHYDRATE: 31 g
DIETARY FIBER: 12 g

SUGARS: 3 g
PROTEIN: 33 g
PHOSPHORUS: 448 mg

EXTRA-EASY DESSERTS

Fresh Pears with Apricot Glaze

SERVES	PREP TIME	COOK TIME
1	5 Minutes	20 Seconds

SERVING SIZE
3/4 cup

3/4 cup sliced pear

2 teaspoons apricot fruit spread

1 teaspoon water

1/8 teaspoon vanilla extract, optional

1/16 teaspoon ground cinnamon (pinch)

1. Place the pears on a dessert plate or shallow bowl.

2. Combine the remaining ingredients in a small microwave-safe bowl. Cook on high setting for 20 seconds or until fruit spread is slightly melted and spoon over pear slices.

CHOICES/ EXCHANGES
1 1/2 Fruit

CALORIES: 90
CALORIES FROM FAT: 0
TOTAL FAT: 0 g
SATURATED FAT: 0 g
TRANS FAT: 0 g

CHOLESTEROL: 0 mg
SODIUM: 0 mg
POTASSIUM: 122 mg
TOTAL CARBOHYDRATE: 23 g
DIETARY FIBER: 3 g

SUGARS: 16 g
PROTEIN: 0 g
PHOSPHORUS: 13 mg

Skillet-Roasted Pineapple and Pear

SERVES
1

PREP TIME
5 Minutes

COOK TIME
3 Minutes

SERVING SIZE
About 3/4 cup

2 teaspoons canola oil

1/2 medium pear, cut into bite-size pieces (about 2/3 cup)

1/2 cup frozen pineapple chunks, thawed and patted dry on paper towels

1/2 teaspoon sugar

1/16 teaspoon ground nutmeg, optional (pinch)

1. Heat the oil in a medium nonstick skillet over medium-high heat, and tilt skillet to coat bottom lightly. Add the fruit in a single layer. Do NOT stir. Cook 3 minutes or until pear is tender-crisp and beginning to lightly brown on the bottom.

2. Stir, remove from heat, sprinkle with sugar and nutmeg, and let stand 1 minute to allow flavors to absorb. Serve warm or at room temperature.

COOK'S NOTE: To thaw frozen pineapple quickly, place pineapple in a microwave-safe bowl, cover, and microwave on high 30–45 seconds.

CHOICES/ EXCHANGES
2 Fruit, 2 Fat

CALORIES: 190
CALORIES FROM FAT: 80
TOTAL FAT: 9 g
SATURATED FAT: 0.5 g
TRANS FAT: 0 g

CHOLESTEROL: 0 mg
SODIUM: 0 mg
POTASSIUM: 103 mg
TOTAL CARBOHYDRATE: 28 g
DIETARY FIBER: 4 g

SUGARS: 13 g
PROTEIN: 1 g
PHOSPHORUS: 11 mg

Sweet Tart Raspberry Phyllo Bites

SERVES	PREP TIME	COOK TIME	STAND TIME
1	5 Minutes	3 Minutes	5 Minutes

SERVING SIZE
5 pieces

2/3 cup frozen raspberries

1 tablespoon strawberry fruit spread

1/8 teaspoon vanilla extract

5 phyllo shells, thawed

2 tablespoons 2% plain Greek yogurt

1. Combine raspberries and fruit spread in a small saucepan, place over medium-high heat, and cook 3 minutes or until mixture has reduced to a scant 1/4 cup.

2. Remove from heat, and stir in extract. Allow to cool, about 5 minutes.

3. Spoon equal amounts in each of the phyllo shells and spoon about 1 teaspoon yogurt over each shell.

COOK'S NOTE: To thaw berries quickly, place frozen berries a microwave-safe bowl and microwave for 15–20 seconds.

CHOICES/ EXCHANGES
1/2 Starch,
1 1/2 Fruit, 1 Fat

CALORIES: 180
CALORIES FROM FAT: 50
TOTAL FAT: 6 g
SATURATED FAT: 0 g
TRANS FAT: 0 g

CHOLESTEROL: 0 mg
SODIUM: 75 mg
POTASSIUM: 85 mg
TOTAL CARBOHYDRATE: 30 g
DIETARY FIBER: 3 g

SUGARS: 12 g
PROTEIN: 3 g
PHOSPHORUS: 0 mg

DESIGNED FOR ONE!

Tender Almond "Baked" Apple

SERVES
1

PREP TIME
5 Minutes

COOK TIME
3 Minutes

STAND TIME
3 Minutes

SERVING SIZE
2 apple halves

1 small apple, halved and cored
(about 5 ounces)

1/2 teaspoon fresh lemon juice

1/8 teaspoon vanilla extract

1/16 teaspoon ground
cinnamon (pinch)

1 tablespoon sliced almonds

1 teaspoon sugar

1. Place apple halves on a microwave-safe plate, and spoon lemon juice and vanilla extract over all. Sprinkle with cinnamon, almonds, and sugar. Cover and microwave on high setting for 3 minutes or until apple is tender-crisp.

2. Remove cover, spoon the drippings over the apples several times , and let stand 2–3 minutes for peak flavors and texture.

> **COOK'S NOTE:** Spooning the drippings over the apple several times allows the drippings to thicken and create its own syrup!

**CHOICES/
EXCHANGES**
1 Fruit,
1 Carbohydrate,
1/2 Fat

CALORIES: 150
CALORIES FROM FAT: 40
TOTAL FAT: 4.5 g
SATURATED FAT: 0 g
TRANS FAT: 0 g

CHOLESTEROL: 0 mg
SODIUM: 0 mg
POTASSIUM: 215 mg
TOTAL CARBOHYDRATE: 27 g
DIETARY FIBER: 4 g

SUGARS: 20 g
PROTEIN: 2 g
PHOSPHORUS: 62 mg

Anytime Banana Split Yogurt

SERVES
1

PREP TIME
5 Minutes

SERVING SIZE
About 1 cup

1/3 cup 2% plain Greek yogurt

1 teaspoon honey

1/2 small banana, sliced
   (1/3 cup)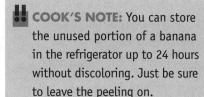

1/3 cup sliced strawberries

1 teaspoon mini semi-sweet
   chocolate chips

1 tablespoon chopped pecans

1. Combine the yogurt and honey in a dessert or soup bowl. Top with the remaining ingredients.

COOK'S NOTE: Before measuring out the honey, lightly coat the measuring spoon with cooking spray, and it will prevent any honey from sticking to the spoon.

COOK'S NOTE: You can store the unused portion of a banana in the refrigerator up to 24 hours without discoloring. Just be sure to leave the peeling on.

**CHOICES/
EXCHANGES**
1 Fruit,
1 Carbohydrate, 1 Lean
Protein, 1 Fat

CALORIES: 200
CALORIES FROM FAT: 70
TOTAL FAT: 8 g
SATURATED FAT: 2 g
TRANS FAT: 0 g

CHOLESTEROL: 5 mg
SODIUM: 25 mg
POTASSIUM: 308 mg
TOTAL CARBOHYDRATE: 28 g
DIETARY FIBER: 3 g

SUGARS: 20 g
PROTEIN: 8 g
PHOSPHORUS: 48 mg

Minted Kiwi and Blueberries

SERVES
1

PREP TIME
10 Minutes

SERVING SIZE
3/4 cup

1 ripe kiwi, peeled and cut in 8 wedges

1/4 cup frozen blueberries, partially thawed

2 teaspoons fresh lime juice

1 teaspoon sugar

1 tablespoon chopped fresh mint

1. Place the kiwi and blueberries in a shallow bowl or rimmed dessert plate. Squeeze the lime overall and sprinkle with the sugar and mint.

2. If time allows, let stand 15 minutes to allow flavors to absorb.

CHOICES/ EXCHANGES
1 Fruit,
1/2 Carbohydrate

CALORIES: 80
CALORIES FROM FAT: 5
TOTAL FAT: 0.5 g
SATURATED FAT: 0 g
TRANS FAT: 0 g

CHOLESTEROL: 0 mg
SODIUM: 0 mg
POTASSIUM: 272 mg
TOTAL CARBOHYDRATE: 20 g
DIETARY FIBER: 3 g

SUGARS: 14 g
PROTEIN: 1 g
PHOSPHORUS: 28 mg

Strawberries with Honey Cream

SERVES
1

PREP TIME
5 Minutes

SERVING SIZE
1 cup

1 cup strawberries, quartered

2 tablespoons light sour cream

1/2 teaspoon honey

1/8 teaspoon vanilla extract or
3–4 drops almond extract

1. Combine all ingredients in a bowl.

COOK'S NOTE: Before measuring out the honey, lightly coat the measuring spoon with cooking spray, and it will prevent any honey from sticking to the spoon.

For Variation: You can combine the sour cream, honey, and extract and serve as a dip alongside whole strawberries.

**CHOICES/
EXCHANGES**
1 Fruit, 1/2 Fat

CALORIES: 100
CALORIES FROM FAT: 25
TOTAL FAT: 3 g
SATURATED FAT: 2 g
TRANS FAT: 0 g

CHOLESTEROL: 10 mg
SODIUM: 25 mg
POTASSIUM: 223 mg
TOTAL CARBOHYDRATE: 16 g
DIETARY FIBER: 3 g

SUGARS: 12 g
PROTEIN: 3 g
PHOSPHORUS: 35 mg

Chocolate Chip–Peanut Butter Apple Slices

SERVES
1

PREP TIME
5 Minutes

COOK TIME
15–20 Seconds

SERVING SIZE
About 3/4 cup apple slices (7–8 apple slices)

1 tablespoon low-fat granola

3/4 cup apple slices

2 teaspoons reduced-fat peanut butter

2 teaspoons fat-free milk

2 teaspoons mini chocolate chips

1. Place the granola in a small baggie, crush to a fine texture, and set aside.

2. Place the apple slices on a dessert plate in a single layer.

3. Combine the peanut butter and milk in a small microwave-safe bowl and microwave on high for 15–20 seconds or until peanut butter has softened. Immediately stir the peanut butter mixture and drizzle it over the apple slices.

4. Sprinkle evenly with the chocolate chips and the crushed granola.

**CHOICES/
EXCHANGES**
1 Fruit,
1 Carbohydrate,
1 Fat

CALORIES: 170
CALORIES FROM FAT: 60
TOTAL FAT: 7 g
SATURATED FAT: 2 g
TRANS FAT: 0 g

CHOLESTEROL: 0 mg
SODIUM: 105 mg
POTASSIUM: 157 mg
TOTAL CARBOHYDRATE: 28 g
DIETARY FIBER: 4 g

SUGARS: 17 g
PROTEIN: 4 g
PHOSPHORUS: 44 mg

Raspberry Softie

SERVES
1

PREP TIME
5 Minutes

CHILL TIME
30 Minutes

SERVING SIZE
1/2 cup

1/3 cup plain 2% Greek yogurt

2/3 cup frozen raspberries, thawed

1 1/2 teaspoons sugar

1/8 teaspoon almond extract or vanilla extract

1. Combine all ingredients in a bowl and mash and stir until smooth. Place in the freezer for 30 minutes for a soft-serve frozen dessert.

COOK'S NOTE: To thaw berries quickly, place frozen berries a microwave-safe bowl and microwave for 15–20 seconds.

CHOICES/ EXCHANGES
1 Fruit,
1/2 Carbohydrate,
1 Lean Protein

CALORIES: 120
CALORIES FROM FAT: 15
TOTAL FAT: 1.5 g
SATURATED FAT: 1 g
TRANS FAT: 0 g

CHOLESTEROL: 5 mg
SODIUM: 25 mg
POTASSIUM: 192 mg
TOTAL CARBOHYDRATE: 21 g
DIETARY FIBER: 3 g

SUGARS: 14 g
PROTEIN: 7 g
PHOSPHORUS: 101 mg

Gingered Blueberry Chiller

SERVES
1

PREP TIME
5 Minutes

STAND TIME
15 Minutes

SERVING SIZE
About 2/3 cup

2/3 cup frozen blueberries

1 1/2 teaspoons sugar

1/2 teaspoon fresh lemon juice

1/4 teaspoon grated ginger

1. Combine all ingredients in a bowl and let stand 15 minutes to thaw slightly and absorb flavors.

**CHOICES/
EXCHANGES**
1/2 Fruit,
1/2 Carbohydrate

CALORIES: 70

CALORIES FROM FAT: 5

TOTAL FAT: 0.5 g

SATURATED FAT: 0 g

TRANS FAT: 0 g

CHOLESTEROL: 0 mg

SODIUM: 0 mg

POTASSIUM: 55 mg

TOTAL CARBOHYDRATE: 18 g

DIETARY FIBER: 3 g

SUGARS: 14 g

PROTEIN: 1 g

PHOSPHORUS: 1 mg

Chunky Mango Gelato

SERVES
1

PREP TIME
5 Minutes

SERVING SIZE
3/4 cup

6 ounces frozen mango (a scant cup), partially thawed ▮

1 teaspoon water or orange juice

1/2 teaspoon vanilla extract

1/4 teaspoon grated orange rind

1. Combine all ingredients in a blender and purée until almost smooth.

▮ **COOK'S NOTE:** To thaw quickly, place mango in a microwave-safe bowl, cover, and microwave on high setting for 30 seconds.

**CHOICES/
EXCHANGES**
2 Fruit

CALORIES: 110
CALORIES FROM FAT: 5
TOTAL FAT: 0.5 g
SATURATED FAT: 0 g
TRANS FAT: 0 g

CHOLESTEROL: 0 mg
SODIUM: 0 mg
POTASSIUM: 291 mg
TOTAL CARBOHYDRATE: 26 g
DIETARY FIBER: 3 g

SUGARS: 23 g
PROTEIN: 1 g
PHOSPHORUS: 24 mg

Espresso Frozen Cherry Yogurt Bowl

SERVES
1

PREP TIME
5 Minutes

SERVING SIZE
About 1 cup

4 ounces frozen dark, sweet cherries (about 3/4 cup)

1/3 cup frozen chocolate yogurt, softened slightly

1/4 teaspoon instant coffee granules

1. Place the cherries in the bottom of the bowl, and top with the yogurt.

2. Using the back of a fork, press the yogurt down gently to allow the yogurt to adhere to the cherries. Sprinkle with the coffee granules.

3. Serve immediately or cover and freeze 25–30 minutes for a soft-serve frozen dessert.

COOK'S NOTE: You may want to double or triple the recipe and make several bowls to keep on hand. It's a great method for portion control, too! To serve from a solid state, let stand on counter about 15 minutes to soften slightly.

CHOICES/ EXCHANGES			
1 Fruit,	CALORIES: 150	CHOLESTEROL: 10 mg	SUGARS: 26 g
1 Carbohydrate,	CALORIES FROM FAT: 20	SODIUM: 35 mg	PROTEIN: 3 g
1/2 Fat	TOTAL FAT: 2 g	POTASSIUM: 136 mg	PHOSPHORUS: 52 mg
	SATURATED FAT: 1.5 g	TOTAL CARBOHYDRATE: 30 g	
	TRANS FAT: 0 g	DIETARY FIBER: 4 g	

Frozen Banana-Pecan Sandwiches

SERVES
3

PREP TIME
10 Minutes

CHILL TIME
2 Hours

SERVING SIZE
1 sandwich

1/4 cup chopped pecans, preferably toasted

1 cup sliced ripe banana, mashed

1/2 teaspoon vanilla extract

3 full sheets low-fat graham cracker, broken in half

1. Stir together the pecans, banana, and vanilla. Spoon equal amounts of the banana mixture on 3 squares, and top with the remaining squares, pressing down very lightly to adhere.

2. Wrap individually in a sheet of foil and freeze until firm, about 2 hours.

COOK'S NOTE: The sandwiches are easy to make and since they may be frozen up to one month, why not make a few more to keep on hand?

CHOICES/ EXCHANGES
1 1/2 Carbohydrate, 1 1/2 Fat

CALORIES: 160
CALORIES FROM FAT: 70
TOTAL FAT: 8 g
SATURATED FAT: 1 g
TRANS FAT: 0 g

CHOLESTEROL: 0 mg
SODIUM: 55 mg
POTASSIUM: 216 mg
TOTAL CARBOHYDRATE: 24 g
DIETARY FIBER: 3 g

SUGARS: 10 g
PROTEIN: 2 g
PHOSPHORUS: 36 mg

No Bake Peanut Butter-Oat Balls

SERVES
1

PREP TIME
5 Minutes

COOK TIME
15–20 seconds

SERVING SIZE
4 balls

2 tablespoons quick-cooking oats

1 1/2 tablespoons reduced-fat peanut butter

1/2 teaspoon honey

1/2 teaspoon fat-free milk

1/16 teaspoon ground cinnamon (pinch)

2–3 drops almond extract, optional

1. Combine all ingredients in a small microwave-safe bowl. Microwave on high setting for 15–20 seconds or until peanut butter has melted slightly. *Do not cook longer or the peanut butter will dry out.*

2. Working quickly, stir until well-blended and form into 4 small balls.

COOK'S NOTE: Before measuring out the honey, lightly coat the measuring spoon with cooking spray, and it will prevent any honey from sticking to the spoon.

CHOICES/ EXCHANGES
1 1/2 Carbohydrate,
1 High Fat Protein

CALORIES: 200
CALORIES FROM FAT: 90
TOTAL FAT: 10 g
SATURATED FAT: 2 g
TRANS FAT: 0 g

CHOLESTEROL: 0 mg
SODIUM: 190 mg
POTASSIUM: 48 mg
TOTAL CARBOHYDRATE: 22 g
DIETARY FIBER: 3 g

SUGARS: 6 g
PROTEIN: 8 g
PHOSPHORUS: 59 mg

Sweet and Nutty Trail Mix

SERVES
1

PREP TIME
5 Minutes

SERVING SIZE
1/2 cup

1/2 ounce salted mini pretzel twists

1 tablespoon chopped pecans

1 tablespoon dried cranberries

2 teaspoons mini semi-sweet chocolate chips

1. Combine all ingredients.

**CHOICES/
EXCHANGES**
1 1/2 Carbohydrate,
1 1/2 Fat

CALORIES: 160
CALORIES FROM FAT: 60
TOTAL FAT: 7 g
SATURATED FAT: 1.5 g
TRANS FAT: 0 g

CHOLESTEROL: 0 mg
SODIUM: 210 mg
POTASSIUM: 74 mg
TOTAL CARBOHYDRATE: 25 g
DIETARY FIBER: 2 g

SUGARS: 12 g
PROTEIN: 2 g
PHOSPHORUS: 40 mg

DESIGNED FOR ONE!

INDEX